Mary P. Sawtelle

The Heroine of 49

a Story of the Pacific Coast

Mary P. Sawtelle

The Heroine of 49
a Story of the Pacific Coast

ISBN/EAN: 9783743313088

Manufactured in Europe, USA, Canada, Australia, Japa

Cover: Foto ©ninafisch / pixelio.de

Manufactured and distributed by brebook publishing software (www.brebook.com)

Mary P. Sawtelle

The Heroine of 49

Mary P. Sawtelle M.D.

ILLUSTRATED BY

ESSIE G. SAWTELLE.

THE HEROINE OF '49

A STORY

OF THE PACIFIC COAST.

By MRS. M. P. SAWTELLE, M. D.

Of San Francisco, Cal.

Copyright, 1891, by Mrs. M. P. Sawtelle, M. D.; in the office of the Librarian of Congress, at Washington.
ALL RIGHTS RESERVED.

PRESS NOTICES OF THE FIRST EDITION.

We herewith return thanks for the many complimentary notcies received from the press, and give a few extracts from some of the leading newspapers:

"The story presents a realistic picture of frontier life in California."—*Chicago Herald.*

"The brave, young heroine, with a courage so sublime as to seem ideal, passes through her tremendous trials, and by lofty courage and indomitable perseverance wins her way to a sweet, noble and successful life."—*Seattle Press-Times.*

"It portrays in a very striking manner some of the evil effects of the law-approved ethics of pioneer days. The entire work is alive with the journalistic touch and genuine newspaper instinct."—*Stockton (Cal.) Mail.*

"Her characters are drawn from real life, and the incidents of the story give a glimpse of domestic life on the Pacific coast during the days of its early settlement. She writes with feeling, and often with power."—*S. F. Bulletin.*

"She has produced a graphic sketch of pioneer days on this coast. The book depicts a life which is now only a memory among the generation that is fast passing away, and, therefore, aside from its ethical purpose, it has a value as a picture of the pioneer days."—*S. F. Chronicle.*

"In her most interesting book, Dr. Sawtelle has given a vivid picture of the conditions which prevailed and which governed society life in the early days on the Pacific coast. All this she has portrayed with a strong, true hand and an unflinching purpose, so that the book stands outside the pale of romance as a social and ethical study of the relations of men and women, of the duty of parents to children, and of the further relation of the government to all its wards. In all that she has treated of, there is a feminine delicacy of truth that makes the book attractive in spirit, while it is none the less strong in purpose."—SALLIE JOY WHITE of *Boston Herald.*

"The book is well worth reading."—*S. F. Evening Post.*

"The material existed for an excellent story, and Dr. Sawtelle certainly has made good use of it. The book is one that will do much good if widely circulated."—*Los Angeles Herald.*

"She writes with dramatic power and tells her story well. The heroine is a high type of American girlhood, and develops into a most charming character of perfect womanhood."—*S. F. News-Letter.*

"A California novel of wide merit—one which points a moral which few authors would assume to point. It has a force and vigor which appeals to the strong mind. A good book that can be profitably read by all."—*Ukiah Press.*

"This tale of pioneer days in California, and of those who cast their lot among the gold-hunters, is pleasantly touched upon and worthy of perusal. The work is a splendid one and should be read by every one, whether pioneers of the golden state or not.'—*St. Helena Star.*

"'The Heroine of '49,' a story by Mary P. Sawtelle, M. D., has met with a large sale, and already a new edition is called for. It will be revised, beautifully illustrated and richly bound. The story is full of interesting incidents, the characters being a young prospector seeking for gold, an Indian maiden, and the usual sturdy persons of a mining camp."—*Argonaut.*

WHAT THE CRITICS SAY.

"Why hold the government to account for infant girls being married to secure land?"

Let the government deal as honorably with its women as its men. If it gives a donation of land to women, why tack on the damaging clause—"all married women?" Is there a case on record where a land law was ever weighed down with the clause—"all married men?"

A matured, brainy physician writes: "I was overwhelmed with rage, from cover to cover, but the book will be read. It will change the laws of property and marriage for women, and will be translated into every civilized tongue."

A minister's wife writes: "Why didn't you make the Indian Caweecha kill Miser?"

For the delectation of the sanguinary critics, the Indian will enact the murder of Miser in the forthcoming drama of "The Heroine of '49."

A learned gentleman writes, desiring to know why we did not write like Shakespeare.

Another one complains that it is "not equal to George Eliot's 'Mill on the Floss' "—another "that it is not as artistic as Helen Hunt Jackson's 'Ramona' "—and all with one accord declare that "Mrs. Murdstone is a fool."

She is a true, representative American mother, my dear lady critics.

Another critic writes: "The best passage in the book, or perhaps in the English language, is where Jean says to her gray-haired friends, whose hearts are true as steel, that '*all the laws and law-makers in the world can't ruin me; I'll still be myself.*'"

Another critic writes: "Why arraign a man before the bar of public opinion for deeds committed forty years ago, when, no doubt, he has repented of them long ago?" If he has repented, let him strip off his befouled ermine, worn so long that the stench reaches to high heaven, and has tainted every other bench in the land, casting a stigma upon the very name of judge, that no poor words of ours, though brewed in bitterest gall, could ever do. Let him pay back the ill-gotten gain to its rightful owners he so basely wronged, and do what poor right is still in his power to do; let him do it now before he enters into the dark unknown, where hissing devils will whisper remorse forever in his ears, and where, before his unrepenting eyes, red-hot fiends will tear clinging babes from tender mothers' arms forevermore.

Preface.

"An eye for an eye, and a tooth for a tooth," is the old Mosaic law that has filled the world with admiration; the equity that admits of no fine balancing or quibbling with the scales of justice—"a consummation devoutly to be wished."

This little work was undertaken with the hope of awakening this sense of equity in regard to our girls, and placing them as nature has done, on a fair footing with their brothers.

People who are stung by the conviction that they have aided in the great wrong of inveigling young maidens into early marriages, will perhaps denounce us as having exceeded the bounds of cool philosophy in our criticism on the early marriages of girls. But the first dawn of reason brought to our mind the full tide of the overwhelming falsehood that girls arrive at the age of maturity sooner than boys—girls being legally of age at eighteen and boys at twenty-one—together with its evil effects upon the individual, as well as upon the whole human race; and "though the heavens fall," we are compelled to speak the truth, and not complacently smile at this monster lie any longer.

The laws governing the property of girls, as well as those of the marriage rites, are based most basely on this idea. The wonder is, that a fact so wide of the truth and fraught with so much evil and not an atom of good, could acquire such a hold on honest people and not find someone to refute it long ago.

We defy any physiologist to find, in the whole realm of nature, an atom of fact that will substantiate the lie that girls grow faster than boys. We defy a person living to bring an instance of one case, from an elephant to a mouse, including the human race, where the parents can produce male offspring that will mature less rapidly than the female offspring. Nature would have to invent a new kind of parentage before she could accomplish this great feat. Let any physician refute this who can, but let him not forget that the author still holds a pen. There are profound physiological laws governing growth and maturity that few people could be made to comprehend. Even the average physician would have to be better versed in physiology than he is, we are sorry to say, before he could grasp these great truths that are before him, working out, with unerring precision, the great laws of growth, maturity and decay.

Just as the last drop of ink is drained from our pen, there comes through the papers a wail from a great statesman, because forsooth, a woman older than his son has inveigled the youth of seventeen into marriage. The blizzard of early marriage seems to have struck the astute stateman hard, making his howl of pain reach from Maine to Oregon. Though thought by some to be the one man of brains in the United States, and though his giant intellect is always bubbling and boiling like the witches' caldron, for the good of the people, yet the comforting thought has never entered his head that "What is sauce for the goose is sauce for the gander."

If every girl in America were married at seventeen, there would not have been such a sensation as has been raised over this seventeen-year-old weakling—because he is a boy and will some day be a man. It would be most absurd for one to suppose for a moment that this great statesman could waste his time in bettering the condition of women. Women! What are women? Nothing but the mothers of men.

We are not a statesman and haven't been attitudinizing for the last thirty years for the highest position in the gift of the people, yet we know enough to tell you that you had better marry your sons a thousand to one, at seventeen, than your daughters at that tender age—and we shall ever pray that the idea may be instilled into the hearts of the people till every parent whose daughter is married at seventeen will be as painfully shocked as this man was at the marriage of his son at that immature age.

The characters in the story are drawn from real life. No living author could have produced them without witnessing the scenes depicted in the work. It covers a new, romantic, broad field. The characters are good and bad, just as they existed; Murdstone being first cousin to Dickens's Murdstone, in *David Copperfield*. Everybody is familiar with that hard character. This Murdstone has, however, with bible in hand, determined to grind some good from out his own character, and there is hope for him. The world is as full of Murdstones as it is of Smiths, and the name should be used oftener to show up that hard type of man. It is the intention of the author to try to make people see the wrong they do to children by beating their flesh to enlighten or cultivate their brains. The thing is vile, and parental authority a crime ten times to one, that should be abolished from families; love only, parental love, guiding the childhood of our nation.

At the request of some upright judges and their friends who thought the name "Boughtup" too suggestive, we have changed the name to Judge Didit. It was never our intention to cast a slur on any honorable court, but we would like to ask, if it is right to thrust a person into jail for contempt of an honest court, then is it not equally right to thrust the whole world into jail if it does not *hold in highest contempt a dishonorable judge?*

Judge Didit and Cursica Miser are characters too often met with, alas, in real life, and if they did not exist as they are portrayed, or act as they are represented, the sun never hung in the heavens.

It is wonderful to note how the transaction of eight

thousand dollars, passing from the one man to the other, left the one in the deepest obscurity, while the other took the money and bloomed out where his dastardly proceedings have made landmarks all along a life brimful of iniquities perpetrated upon his fellows.

Feeling the necessity of a historic sketch giving at least a glimpse of the family life of the first settlers on the Pacific Coast, this work was undertaken with the hope that possibly its incompleteness may be the means of inspiring some one to write a more perfect and complete account of this period, knowing how soon time obliterates every vestige of the past; believing full well that a time will come when a people enjoying the magnificence and marvelous wealth of these Pacific States will look back with hearts filled with gratitude to the people who laid the foundation for it all, made sacrifices and endured privations that would be difficult for any historian, however accurate or gifted, to portray, and any account of those days, however imperfect, will be held sacred by them forever.

THE AUTHOR.

THE HEROINE OF '49.

CHAPTER I.

JEWELS OR NO JEWELS.

It was the winter of 1871 in New York City. We were at dinner in the richly draped, warm dining-room of the brownstone-front mansion of the banker Barron. The cheerful warmth of the room contrasted strongly with the outside sleet and snow that was just beginning to fall; it gave a soft glow to the silken draperies and bright mirrors that served as doors on the china closets, and extended from ceiling to floor, reflecting the warm light of the fire, the stately clock above it that told of the flight of time in a chime of bells, and the fine, old, carved oaken side-board, with its antique Persian ewer and tray of exquisite beauty, and its dainty blue and gold china; for Mr. Barron was not a poor banker—he was a millionaire.

Jean Reming had been at the home of her queenly sister-in-law a whole week, stupid mortal, and had not observed that in eating soup (if such esthetic mortals could be said to eat soup and not absorb it) they dipped the soup away from them instead of towards them in conveying it to the mouth. We had finished soup, however, and fish and fowl had been brought, and Mr. Barron was carving with that ease that comes only with practice. Madam Barron sat waiting, resplendent in her beauty and jewels, flashing her wit at Jean Reming. She said: "You will write a story and put us all in it—the bears of the Sierras and the bankers of New York." And Mr. Barron remarked: " Bears are good to write about, I am sure. I have just bought a fine skin for a carriage robe that is rich, black and glossy." " Perhaps," said Madam, " Mr. Barron will lend you the robe to enable you to give a more accurate description of the bears." " Oh, that would be tame indeed," said Jean, brightly. " I shall have real wild bears, perhaps not in ' droves of five hundred,' as Sam Slimmins describes them in ' Picturesque Sierras,' but one, now and again, roaming in dignified solitude, helping himself to acorns—a harmless, proper creature enough when you do not venture to encroach upon his dominions. My ideal bear would never wander into this great city and molest you."

" What is the title of your book to be, Jean?" inquired Madam Barron.

" Now, really, I do not know what to call the book; it's the most puzzling question I will have to grapple with," answered Jean, feeling that she was being laughed at, and wishing that Madam had her dinner on her plate so that she could give her attention to that and not be able to talk any more, when to Jean's relief, Madam said, with a little laugh, " I have it, I will help you this much, call it ' Why is this Thus?'"

"Good enough," answered Jean with a smile. " The book, if it is ever written, shall be called by your title."

" How soon shall you publish it?" asked Mr. Barron, " I have promised Mark Steger that I will take one hundred copies of his book that he is writing, entitled ' How Will it End?' and I will do as well by you."

" I shall be proud to have so good a reader, and will order the bookseller to send you a hundred copies," said Jean, plunging into her dinner with an appetite that her sister-in-law's banter had only sharpened.

The two sisters-in-law were as unlike as could well be. Madam Barron was a woman of thirty years, with steel-gray eyes, dark hair, a Grecian nose, perfect features, and a complexion that rivaled a rose in its fine tones. She was stately in her carriage, with a touch of languor scarcely definable, and yet when you came to know her, you would see that this love of ease entered largely into her character, giving strong color to all her acts. Her dress was of soft, pearl-gray silk, one of Worth's, costing anywhere between three and five hundred dollars. On her well-poised head, with its wealth of rich, dark hair, hovered a dainty gold butterfly, with eyes of costly diamonds, its outspread wings seeming to flutter against her braids; diamonds fastened soft lace at her throat.

Madam Barron had been a poor girl, too, in her childhood, but she had an ambitious aunt, who thought it cheaper to spend one summer at Saratoga than to care for her handsome niece many summers in the humdrum town they lived in. Sure enough, one outing did the business. Mr. Barron saw the beautiful Celia at the opening ball of the season, danced with her twice, and every mamma there decided the g... had won her prize before the evening closed, and the gay throng had passed from the bright scene into oblivion, to be again reunited, walking, driving, boating, dancing again. O, the happy, merry time! Mr. Barron had only a few days to spend from his business. Celia was far too pretty a girl to leave untrammeled by an engagement. Her aunt was interviewed, Celia sought, and a carefully arranged engagement made. Mr. Barron always declared that he had to make love to his wife all their married life because he had had no time to do the usual amount of courting before, and surely he always looked the lover and she the happy bride. The aunt was the happiest mortal alive, saying often:

"Supposing I had kept that splendid creature hid up in that mountain village of Tuckertown, you would never have had such a wife."

"O, yes, I should," declared Mr. Barron. "I never

would have married any other girl than your niece, Mrs. Mulford. I'd have gone fishing for trout in Tuckertown mill-ponds," heartily insisted Mr. Barron, "but I should have found Celia."

The only thing that could be said to mar the appointment of their elegant home and the seeming happiness of their marriage was that there never came any little Barrons and Barronesses to add to their great happiness; so to amuse themselves, they played that Jean's little golden-haired Dot was their very own, when mamma Jean was not near to hear. The little lady would enter into the fun with as much zest as her uncle and auntie did. They adopted her in their hearts, bought her dresses that suited her type of beauty, and petted her without stint. Every day her loveliness increased, and she grew more charming in her childlike ways. All their fondness and caressing, however injudiciously lavished upon her, instead of spoiling her, only brought out the more her sweet and tender nature, as she nestled in the hearts of all who saw her. Dot had hair like spun gold in the sunlight. It fell in heavy waves all over her shoulders, reaching below her sash, where it clustered in great heavy ringlets that would have delighted the soul of a Titian. Amie, the French maid, might brush it ever so straight, and in a two minutes' romp it would curl up in those great, luscious curls at the ends, in the most bewitching way. Dot had large eyes like her mother, but they were blue, like her Auntie Barron's. Her nose was slightly *retroussé*, with broad nostrils that indicated good breathing capacity, and insures to any animal good health. She had chubby cheeks and a funny little mouth that she could kiss very sweetly with, and with which she played the diplomat in the most remarkable way; these kisses deciding whether she should be a poor little girl and live with Mama Jean all her life, or be the sole heiress of her Uncle Barron, and always stay with Auntie

JEWELS OR NO JEWELS.   13

Barron. Dot was a tall child for her five years, as well rounded in limb and firm of flesh as any young filly that ever won a race. No sculptor could ask for a finer model; there was strength, endurance, delicacy, perfection. The soft, velvety skin, glowing with health, was not too white, but gave promise that a tinge of the olive from Mamma Jean's dark eyes, hair and skin, would assert itself in the little lady, and make for her a wealth of rarest beauty when she grew to womanhood. All the ills that children are usually tormented with had touched her lightly, as water touches a duck's back, and rolled off, much the same way, leaving her bright, fresh, sunny as a great luscious La France rosebud, giving promise of a long, strong, happy life, as a morn in August gives promise of sunshine.

One evening as Madam Barron and Jean sat alone in the library, Madame said in confidential, sisterly tones: "Jean, my dear, I never in my life saw a hand and arm so exquisitely molded as yours is," and Jean raised her big brown eyes and answered in charming frankness: "You surprise and please me. If you were anybody else, my dear sister, I should think that you were flattering. If I have a grain of vanity about me you have touched it. Our family historian has lately chronicled the fact that our English grandmothers were fond of their shapely fingers, and really I think it is something to be proud of."

"Indeed, Jean, you should wear jewels," said Mrs. Barron; and poor Jean looked up with her great eyes a little saddened and answered:

"Oh, I never could."

Mrs. Barron thought that she meant she could not afford the expense of jewels, and said:

"Oh, never mind, my dear, I am going to Tiffany's next week to get some beautiful diamonds, and as I have so many myself, I shall deem it a great favor if you will accept them."

"I appreciate your kindness, my dear sister. I fear

you do not understand me. I cannot wear jewels. My nerves are sensitive. Perhaps I may be possessed of the same feeling that men have about jewels; you see, yourself, they do not wear them," said Jean in her directness, being half afraid, all the while, that she would offend Madam Barron, and so went on—

"I think, I get as much enjoyment in seeing other women wearing ornaments, and, perhaps, more than they do. I enjoy the sparkle of diamonds," and was just about to add that she did not like to see ornaments in the ears, but remembering in time, that Madam Barron had worn such heavy rings in her ears that one had worn its way through the lobe of the ear leaving a horrid deformity, she refrained from saying that she thought it was a piece of barbarity to have holes pierced in the flesh for the purpose of attaching ornaments to the person.

"Don't allow me to impress you with the idea that I do not wish to appear well—no ones cares more for personal attractiveness than I," said Jean quietly, "but it is impossible for me to wear gold bands pressing on the delicate tissues of my fingers. I have tried it, and they suffocate me. I am sensitive. I like soft laces, and light, warm cashmeres to touch my flesh—something like those worn by the women of the Orient would suit me." Jean was feeling that she was getting farther and farther from her sister-in-law's idea of what was proper for women of culture and refinement to wear, and so she queried:

"If I had all the jewels in Tiffany's great storehouse, what do you think I would do with them? I would sell them, as he does, but I would not take the money and buy more. I would build a great work-house, a sort of emergency establishment, where the laboring classes when they were thrown out of employment would find work and be sure of their daily bread, until they could get their old work back again or secure better occupation; where women who had lost their husbands, and had young children to support, could be employed until they could find more remunerative business. I would have great work-shops, where boys and girls could learn how to become skilled laborers, and, if I were our great national government, I would build this kind of establishment in every state in the Union, jewels or no jewels."

Madame Barron sat waiting, resplendent in her beauty and jewels, flashing her wit at Jean Reming.

CHAPTER II.

JEAN REMING.

Jean Reming was a firmly-built, compact woman, of medium size, with very large hazel-brown eyes. Her queenly pose impressed one that she was a much larger woman than she really was. Her strength of character diffused itself about her like an atmosphere—you felt it as you feel the brightness of a June day, or the breeze of an ocean sea-side. If she stepped into a brilliant social company, all eyes were upon her; if into a legislative body of statesmen, each great man armed his wit with a keener edge, found words to convey his subtlest meaning, feeling sure that the deep, brown, soulful eyes of Jean Reming would fathom his profoundest thought, if no one else did.

When Jean was a mere maiden, and lived on the border of those vast forests of the Pacific Coast, where rolled the mighty Oregon, and heard naught save its own dashings, the Indian was touched by the same feeling, something akin to awe, and on two or three occasions, this power of Jean's had prevented an outbreak of the savages. The Indian, with heart raging with all the untrained passions of hatred and revenge for the pale-faced foe, had been subdued into burying his tomahawk, and wheeling into good behavior, simply by the presence of this young girl at the door of his wigwam. The untamed soul of the desperate savage was made to feel that it was better to look for a day of deliverance by appealing to the better part of his foe than by total extermination of the whites who were trespassing on his landed estates which he held by inheritance in fee simple.

Jean called this power her fate. She hated to be

observed, and since her earliest recollection, it had been her misfortune to be. It made her retiring and careful, both to a degree. Her movements, if studied, were almost classical in grace, her smile was only a bright ripple that scarcely moved a muscle of her fine oval face, and quickly faded into a Madonna-like sadness.

Jean Reming, when a child was an only daughter of Benjamin Ames, a clergyman who had five sons. It may seem strange that Jean should come nearer taking the place of her father, when he died while the children were all small, than any of the sons.

The older sons, as it often happens, had to rustle for themselves; so it came about that Jean should be the prop of her mother whose constant companion she was. Alfred, the youngest, was an infant only one year old, Will seven and Jean nine; the other two boys, Ben and Tom, twelve and fourteen. The eldest son had been left at school in New England. The Ameses had immigrated to this country only the year before.

Mrs. Ames was a New England wife and mother; left on the broad prairie of an Illinois rented farm, when her husband, dying, left her with a narrow income strangely inadequate to the almost unlimited necessities of a vigorously growing family. The mother was a well-bred lady. Her thorough education stood her well in the stirring time of her great need. She was wholly untrained to do business, however. Jean Ames, being the idol of the house, her mother was afraid her daughter would grow up boyish, because she was the only girl among so many boys. But if there had been five daughters instead of one, Jean's nature would have asserted itself just the same. Mr. Ames was a man of education, and knowing that he would be away from home preaching, always kept everything in order about the place. So Mrs. Ames decided to remain on the farm with her little ones until the following spring, as the wood was all piled up under the shed for the long winter's use—walnut and hickory logs, the best wood that was ever put into a big, old-fashioned, open-faced fireplace in the world to throw out a bright blaze, drying the snow from the boy's feet or making you ashamed to let a tear glisten on your face even for so great a loss as a husband and father—father of such a promising flock as the little Ameses were. And then the feed was all stowed away in the big barn for the horses, cows, sheep and young cattle; corn for the cackling hens, waddling ducks and clamoring geese. The hogs were being fattened, everything in readiness for the king of winter's sure coming, when alas! the king of terror had swept away the father so suddenly, giving only four days' warning. The neighbors had all decided that it was a very foolish thing for Mrs. Ames to try to stay on the farm all winter—that she ought to sell out everything she could and give away the rest and go back to her family in the East. A Mr. Teet, living near, came in to say that as she was left in so helpless a condition with her little ones, he would take home her fattest hog in the pen, kill it and bring her back all the hog; he keeping the head, feet and offal for his trouble. Mrs. Ames smiled at the odd proposition, saying: "I fear that will be poor pay for your trouble, Mr. Teet."

"Oh, Mrs. Ames, I shall not mind doing you a kindness; the bible tells us to be good to the widow and fatherless."

Mrs. Ames wiped away a tear she could not repress at hearing her little ones spoken of in this helpless way; she could scarcely realize the fact yet, as her husband was often away from home, and to her it seemed he must come back. In a moment she recovered and said.

"If you will prepare the pig for meat, Mr. Teet, I shall be very glad. Mr. Rogers was going to send his hired man over Saturday to kill and dress the pig, but your kind offer will save us from an obligation to Mr. Rogers."

Mr. Teet brought back the pig next morning. If anyone could have looked at that circumvented porcine without laughing, he would have to be interested in the meat question of the family, as Jean was. Mrs. Ames looked at the remnants of the curtailed pig and then at Mr. Teet, who was looking as though he thought for the first time that possibly he had taken the lion's share from the widow and orphans, and as though he might say that the pig had shrunk somewhat since the morning before when he took it away, and remarking rather apologetically: "You know, Mrs. Ames, the pig did not weigh so much as we thought it would when it was in the pen." Our meanest acts never look quite so bad to us as when some one else is looking at them with us.

The children had gathered about the table, laughing—who could help it? Ben, bursting into the kitchen, said: "Well, Ma, I think the pig's head is cut off just behind the shoulder, and the tail up to the shoulder."

Mrs. Ames was looking seriously at the pig and Mr. Teet alternately. Jean was not ten years old, but she knew her mother would say nothing to the man who had so imposed upon them, and indeed what good would words do. Little Jean was not so wise a person as her mother, however, so she stepped in front of Mr. Teet, saying, with a directness that made him quail: "Why didn't you take all the pig?" Now the pig would have weighed one hundred and fifty pounds when Mr. Teet took it away in his wagon, and he brought it back weighing fifty pounds, in a small bag which he carried with ease on his shoulder.

Ben, a boy of fourteen, with his brown curls pushed back from a massive brow, with cheeks round and red as an apple, exclaimed with an impatient air, "Mother, I think it is degrading to let a person swindle you that way."

"Well, my child, very true, but what can you do?"

"Nothing now, mother, but pocket our humiliation, and look out for the next benevolently inclined hypocrite."

CHAPTER III.

THE BOYS' GAME CLUB.

Ben Ames was both an active and scholarly little fellow. He read history, to the great satisfaction of his mother and the children, on dark, rainy nights. But when the beautiful snow, together with the clear, cold moon, made the hunting grounds almost as light as day, Ben, with the boys of the game club, went out hunting coon and rabbit, and the talk of these boys of bringing down bears, deer and wild turkey was much more plentiful than the game itself, although the boys really did bring in game now and again, to the great surprise of themselves and the old folks at home. In those days the prairies of the West abounded with deer and wild turkey.

It turned out that the fun-loving old nigger Johnson captured the coons for the boys, and the club bought the turkeys of some more fortunate hunter and distributed the sports and the honors as they could, without being found out.

As winter was well advanced, one morning there was great excitement over a delicious, fat wild turkey hanging high in the wood-shed at the Ames's. When Jean asked Ben who shot the turkey, "He or Joe Rogers?" Ben said, "Neither of us, and you needn't ask, Miss, for we boys have a rule in the club that we shall not tell who shoots the game, for some of the boys who never shoot anything—but their guns off—don't like it, that's a fact," with a little strut across the floor, adding: "Girls could not make a rule like that, because they would tell, every time; girls cannot keep a secret."

"No," blurted out Jean; "girls don't have secrets to keep, is the reason."

"Children! children!" exclaimed Mrs. Ames, who had heard more of this dialogue than either of the children supposed, "you ought to be quite happy over the turkey without caring who killed it. But I suppose your sister wishes you to carry off the honors of the club as you do those of the spelling-school," added she, soothingly, to Ben.

"No," cried Jean, "I don't want him to get any honors at all, if he struts so, and says such spiteful things about girls, that are not true, either."

"My dear child," replied Mrs. Ames, 'you got the best of your brother when you said girls had no secrets to keep, and I should think that ought to satisfy you."

"And I should think so too," said Ben, " but girls never know when they do score a point, just because we boys don't flinch when we're hit."

Mrs. Ames suspected there was something troubling Ben's conscience a little, so she said, "You may bring home some of the boys from school to-night, Ben, and we'll eat the turkey and have some fun indoors and not go hunting to-night."

Ben was pulling on two long mittens and came back to his mother where she still sat at the breakfast table, giving her a rousing hug, and a kiss that sounded like a pop-gun, saying: "I will bring Will Niles, for he is the best boy in school. How many boys can I bring, mother—six?"

"No," cried Jean, "only three!"

That morning Mrs. Ames sat thinking. While she washed and dressed the smaller children, curled little Alfred's soft brown hair over her fingers—her sweet child treasure—the tears would come, but she wiped them quickly away with the corner of little Alfred's apron and kissed his curls. She was so unused to crying. The tears that had come to her eyes were tears of sympathy; she had so often told women with like affliction of the dear Father's love, that she tried to think the same for herself now, but found it a little harder to see the silver lining behind this cloud that had bereft her of her husband.

Mrs. Ames knew no more of the little deceptions and harmless tricks of the great social circles than she did of the chicanery and fraud practiced in the business world.

She read in her Bible that there was good and evil, but so far the evil had been far from her. The telegraph and daily newspaper did not herald the sins of the whole earth as they do to you and me, dear reader. For herself, she had only dwelt on the goodness of God and his infinite mercies. Her whole life had been a hymn of praise, her thoughts of purity and heaven.

There are tricks that damage the character more than a lie—an outspoken, frank, sturdy, stand-up-and-face-it lie. This thought, not clearly defined, but there just the same, had saddened and set Mrs. Ames to thinking, and this thought saddens and sets the whole world of mothers to thinking, without very much available good coming from it either.

Think what it would be if we were all honest and acted the clean truth. There never would be another house of correction built to put little children in; never another prison where, as Byron says, "man first penned his brother man." Our great national institutions—the dark blot on our civilization—known as our penitentiaries, costing our state governments millions and millions annually to conduct them, would all be turned into great thriving work-shops, where honest labor would ennoble the toilers, and not taint them with a stigma that is bitter and more galling to the higher nature of man than the iron manacles of these institutions that lacerate his flesh.

All the great cities of the world could do without their army of policemen. Look at the immense expense of the one item of bars and bolts and locks and keys all over the world, to say nothing of the great iron safes, and the eternal watch and ward that everybody has to keep over the merest trifle of any value. Think of the millions that are destroyed every year by the incendiary's midnight torch. Think of the time spent in shopping; if you buy a spool of thread to sew a button on Johnny's breeches, you are obliged to sit on a stool ten minutes, and wait for the spool to go meandering around somewhere and come back again, all because an honest clerk cannot be found, or, at least, not a whole store full of honest clerks.

Think of the mighty engine of the giant law, thundering out its vengeance in eternal jaw. Besides all the lawyer's wrangle—consider the time spent sitting, waiting—waiting—waiting for the law's delay; all the honest people as well as the rascals mixed up in the interminable wrangle, until you can't tell one from the other. It is time for somebody to call a halt, and say, "Let us be honest."

We are proud to say that we are a nation of thieves and liars, and every act of our lives and all our business transactions are conducted on this basis. Now, why is this?

It is the first few drops of water that weaken the dam, and unchecked go on and cause a flood. It is the first little defect in our character that makes us at last the great defaulter. It was just this almost untarnishable touch of deceit that rasped Ben on to irritability at the mere mention of who shot the turkey. Mrs. Ames felt sure that Ben was not quite satisfied with himself, and felt savage with anyone who was going to make the discovery of a flaw in his conduct, and she, of all persons, was not going to see his fault, but if Ben brought the boys home to dinner, she was sure that they themselves would disclose it, notwithstanding the boasted superiority of masculine secretiveness.

Mrs. Ames prepared that dinner with as much care and ceremony as if the company were all to be church deacons and archbishops. It had been one of her chief delights to entertain, so it was no great trouble to receive such a bright troop of young gentlemen. She had the knack of dispensing "those simple pleasures that always please" with so much matronly grace that no prince was ever prouder of his mother than Ben. Mrs. Ames thought there never was such a splendid company of boys, so full of manly dignity, so finely balancing the fun, that, in spite of their efforts to control, would every now and again, burst out into uproarious laughter; in fact, they were very unlike the boys in the poem—instead of the forty boys behaving like one, each boy behaved like forty.

Mrs. Ames sat carving the turkey, putting a generous slice of roast pork on every boy's plate. That dressing and those mashed potatoes seasoned with cream and butter, that delicious dish of apple-sauce that went to every boy's plate to be eaten with the roast pork! Then came the pumpkin pie, the walnuts and hickory nuts and big red apples; the stories about how Jean climbed the trees and helped shake those hickory nuts off, and was no more afraid than a boy. And then more fun, until you would think that such a laugh after such a dinner would be dangerous. But the funniest fun of all the fun popped out of Dick Martin's mouth, in a voice loud enough to be heard above all the other boys, after the last delicious mouthful of that splendid bird had been swallowed by that young gentleman.

"Mike Finnegan was a good fellow to shoot this turkey when it was eating old Patton's corn, and then give it to us boys for our game club. Hey, boys, I propose a toast and three cheers. 'May his good aim always bring down as good game, and his generous soul meet with equal generosity from all mankind!'" The boys were on their feet in a moment, giving hearty cheers to that toast. Jean glanced at her mother who sat smiling triumphantly at the boys' method of keeping secrets, and glad in her heart that the little deception that tempted them was no greater. She thought, as the last good-night had been said, that a grander deed could not well be done than to help steer such boys into the clear paths of rectitude that would lead to lives of honor. So she asked Ben the next morning if it would not be a good idea to propose a new rule at the next game-club meeting that would not prove such a strain on the boys' secretiveness. Ben, with another hearty kiss, promised her that he would at their very next meeting, saying:

"And if I just mention that you suggested it, mother, it will be carried without a dissenting voice."

Ben had no opportunity of remedying his game-club law, however, for before they met again he had an offer from the village editor to come into his office and learn to set type.

Ben and Mrs. Ames went to town soon after, talked over the affair with the editor and his wife, for Ben was to live with the family until he was twenty-one years of age, then to go into partnership with the firm, as one of the editors. The saddest time in a mother's life came to Mrs. Ames early—the time when the boys leave home to make their own way in the world.

Thomas, who was two years younger than Ben and not nearly so strong, took largely to books, with very little disposition for gunning.

CHAPTER IV.

THE PROPOSAL.

The minister that took charge of the church after the death of Mr. Ames, proposed to take Thomas, send him to school, and if he should continue in his studious habits, when he became older he would train him for the ministry. So, after many tears and prayers for the dear Father's guidance, Mrs. Ames gave up her boys.

These boys, with their early training, were a source of income to these men, and of course the widow would be relieved of all such burdens. If she had been brave, and kept those splendid boys, and stayed on the farm that had been leased her for a number of years, how much better for them and for her!

The dear snuggery, where lingered all the sweet memories of the last days with husband and father, had to be broken up. Mrs. Ames took a small cottage, and she, Jean, Will, and Alfred were soon settled in the same little town with the boys. One night, after they were all snugly fixed in their new home, Jean and her mother sat sewing by the fireside, Jean threading all the needles. She put the last one down in a long row on the cushion, and said, in a plaintive voice:

"O, mother, why did you not arrange to have the boys sleep at home? It would be like old times to have them come home at night; it's so lonesome this way."

Then Jean was so sorry she had said it, for her mother gave a great sob for an answer. Jean was beside her mother in a moment, with her arms about her neck.

"Mother, mother, do not cry so. I am here; I will

stay with you always. Everybody's boys have to go out and work, don't they, mother? It is not so bad, as they are so near, and we see them every few days. They will soon be men, and have homes of their own; then we will all live together again."

"O, you poor child," sobbed her mother. "How little you know of the ways of the world." But she stopped crying, bathed her face in cold water, glanced into the glass, and wondered if one with such a heart-ache could look only eighteen, as Mr. Sneekinswine had said she did that day when she was in the tailor shop of Messrs. Sneekinswine & Brassfielder, getting her week's work of sewing. Mrs. Ames was mistress of her needle. Emerson has said there is a compensation for everything—was it so now? The fine stitching and embroidery she had done for the infant throng that had come right along without any interruption year after year all her married life; the fine cloth clothes for her little boys which she had often constructed out of their father's old ones, had at least kept her fingers deft at the work.

Messrs. Sneekinswine & Brassfielder had soon found that the men's suits made by Mrs. Ames brought higher prices than those made by their own workmen. But they never offered Mrs. Ames any of the profit brought to them by her good work. They, in fact, kept very still about her doing good work, and even had been mean enough at one time to find some flaw in her sewing. The only way she suspected that she did better work than any one else sewing for the same house was that they insisted upon her taking home the finest cloth suits that they had to make.

It was on one occasion, when Mr. Sneekinswine had asked her to take two suits of fine black broadcloth and have them returned by the next Saturday. The suits were intended for a bridegroom and his best man. Mrs. Ames had said: "Give me the light tweed, if you please, Mr. Sneekinswine, I can sew on that at night, and it will not be so trying to my eyes."

Mr. Sneekinswine had said, with a quizzical smile: "You do not look more than eighteen, Mrs. Ames."

Mrs. Ames did not glance at him, and whatever meaning he might have had was utterly lost upon her, as she firmly replied: "Send the light tweed and the black suit to my house, as I am going to the next store," and she walked quickly out.

The fact had got abroad that Mrs. Ames did fine work. One law firm and two or three doctors had ordered suits made by her; they not paying her quite as much as they would pay the firm of Sneekinswine & Brassfielder, but still, more than that firm would allow her if they had had the order; and knowing this fact, she had felt a strong disposition to walk out of that house and never return, but not being quite sure that she could get custom-work enough to support her children, and knowing that it was a woman's prerogative to avoid any little pleasantry that might or might not be intended as an insult, she determined to keep quiet and try all the harder to get custom-work, and so be independent of this firm as soon as possible.

When Mrs. Ames arrived home an hour later, she found the black and tweed suits awaiting her. Laying off her bonnet and tying a long white apron over her neatly fitting black cashmere dress, she untied the work and assorted it in piles on a long, clean, white pine table; the pants by themselves, the vests by themselves, and each coat in a pile by itself. She took a sleeve of the black cloth coat and commenced sewing as if the long unbroken seam would give her more time for quiet thinking. Stitch, stitch, stitching; for you must not forget that the sewing machine was not invented, and at that period a woman could sit gracefully, stitch quietly and think profoundly; if she had a mind to.

And this is what she thought: If I do not take my eyes off this sewing for two days and a half, and give myself only ten minutes for each meal, I can get the black coat done in that time; the black pants and vest will take two days more; then I have a day and a half of daylight to finish the tweed suit, and make the button holes. Almost the entire suit will have to be made evenings, and I shall be compelled to sit up 'till twelve o'clock every night, and then the pay is a miserable pittance.

Just at this point of her soliloquy there was a rap at the door, and the face of the family physician, dear old Doctor Knight, beamed upon her like the dawn of a new day. He sat down and told her of the probable health and probable death of his numerous patients, adding in a cheery voice, "but, Mrs. Ames, I have a much more thrilling theme to talk to you about," but with his eyes cast down, "you look so cosy and comfortable here I hardly dare to tell you, and you have plenty of work to do, too, I see," glancing at the piles of work laid out on the long table.

Mrs. Ames answered: "Yes, too much work, but not enough pay."

"Well, that gives me heart again, and I'll pluck up courage and tell you, he continued. You know my friend, Murdstone, who lost his wife about a year or ten months ago. He is a member of our church. You perhaps remember seeing his wife; a very quiet, odd little woman, quite pale; she dressed the children so like little old men and women when she brought them to church; didn't know how to sew any more than a mud turtle. She was a Virginia lady, always accustomed to slaves. Well, Murdstone married her when she was quite young, and brought her out to this new country about ten years ago. She brought an old colored servant with her who did what work was done. Mrs. Murdstone never liked the people here. I guess she never spoke ten words in all those ten years to any one except the servant and nurse that came when her children were born. I have attended her with all her children, and at her last confinement she died and left a little girl not an hour old. A sad case. Murdstone took it very hard, poor fellow. He is left with those five little children. He has a snug little home out there six miles in the country, but everything is going to rack and ruin, he tells me. Murdstone is not a bad looking man when you come to that. You know he is a big tall fellow, though he is not a rich man and never will be—not speculative at all, and so most likely will never be a poor man. He is one of those plodding, steady-going kind of men, with not a particle of romance about him.

The quick sympathy of Mrs. Ames had been following his recital. She had often listened to the stories of the doctor's patients, and no more thought that the doctor was getting around to a proposal of marriage between Mr. Murdstone and herself, than she thought of taking a trip to the North Pole. The doctor could see this and it made it all the more difficult for him to get at the pith of his story.

"As I was saying, he is a plain, blunt man, Mrs Ames; no more like your husband was, than a gray dull morning is like the noon-day sun, but then you have brightness and sunshine enough in your nature for two families."

Mrs. Ames raised her great brown eyes full upon him, and said: "What do you mean, Doctor Knight?"

"I mean that those four little, motherless girls need just such a mother as you are, and that Mr. Murdstone is coming into town with a load of grain to mill next week, and he requested me to call upon you and ask you if he might call and see you while his grist is being ground."

Mrs. Ames laughed heartily, saying:

"That is romantic, I am sure, for a man to call upon a lady and ask her to be his wife while the family flour is being ground for the year. I suppose he will propose?" she added in her bright sparkling voice.

"Well, yes," replied the doctor, "I think he will, and you may as well think it all over and be prepared with your answer."

THE PROPOSAL.

"Well, I am glad it is next week he is coming, for I could not give him ten minutes of this week for this sewing."

"I see; you are stitching away with lightning speed."

"Yes, these are busy times. Mr. Murdstone will not make a long call, will he? How long will it take his grist to grind, doctor?"

"The question is not so much about the length of the call as the answer you give him, my dear," a little seriously. "If you were my own sister I could not be more regretful of an unhappy marriage for you, especially since I have been the one to recommend it."

"Indeed," replied Mrs. Ames, "this does look serious."

The doctor rose to go, saying, "Tell me, my dear, I am to see patients to-morrow near Mr. Murdstone's, and if you don't object to his calling, I will say so for you."

"It is a very delicate matter to make answer to, but I will not refuse to see him, however, if he calls."

And the doctor's carriage was soon heard rolling away, and Mrs. Ames' stitching went on as steadily as though the doctor had not called.

CHAPTER V.

THE UNWELCOME VISITOR.

But her thoughts were turned in an entirely different channel. Her heart was especially tender towards the infant brood of little girls. How she felt for her own darlings out in the cold world among strangers, who cared only for the amount of work they could drive them through, subject to harsh criticism, untempered by parental love. If Mrs. Ames had not been at work herself, the meanness of sordid selfishness would not have come home so keenly to her as it did. The very idea of these children, that would have appalled another woman, was the center of attraction to her. If the doctor had not awakened her sympathy for the little motherless ones, she would have said positively and unconditionally, "No; he cannot call, even while his grist is being ground." Now, she thought, he can be a father to my little boys and I can be a mother to the girls. There will be a big family; ten children! How much wisdom will be required to train, direct and rear ten children; his baby only one year old, her's but three. What a nursery! how she would try to be a real mother to the whole infant band, if it should be God's will to place her in that responsible position. No matter what Mr. Murdstone's proposal might be when he came to mill, she would listen to no proposal that did not insure her having all her children with her again. There must surely be plenty of work on the farm, and the boys would be far removed from the evil influences of a small town, where there were always more or less bad elements.

She knew the work for such a large family would be

something enormous, but the love and gratitude of so many little hearts would be something great also. The wail of poor, old King Lear, of, "how sharper than a serpent's tooth it is to have a thankless child," did not enter into her plans for the future of these children."

Mrs. Ames's brain was as busy as her fingers that week. She made plans and resolves that she, for her part, carried out to the letter through a long and eventful life. But the plans she made for others woefully miscarried, as we shall see as we pass on through the coming events of this history.

Mrs. Ames was surprised and annoyed, if not alarmed, at a call from Mr. Sneekinswine the very next day after Doctor Knight's visit. That gentleman seemed so utterly unconscious of the embarrassment he was occasioning, so supremely obtuse to anybody's discomfort, that Mrs. Ames assumed as much indifference to his presence as she well could, and stepping to the other side of the long work-table, stood with folded hands awaiting his orders. It never entered her mind that she could attribute his call to any other object than some direction about the work, and as neither of the firm had ever called upon her before, she was still puzzled, and when he hesitated she inquired: "Why am I honored with a call from you, Mr. Sneekinswine? Perhaps some directions about the work."

"Well, yez; ve vished ferry much to haf it done dees veek."

Mrs. Ames replied: "I have never disappointed your firm in sending the work home at the time I had promised it."

"Yez, and dare is sumding elze, Meesis Ames. Dos little shildren will all shtarve, as already not much more vork goes out ov our house. Mrs. Smith, with her seex shmall shildren, gets no more vork. She ees vurtuous, but her shildren vos go hungry. Dot don't feed dem."

With unnecessary excitement Mr. Sneekinswine

arose from his chair and walked to the table, and leaning towards Mrs. Ames, took up the black broadcloth coat and stuck his clumsy finger through a button-hole that gleamed with its firm silken stitches.

"You vork like dot ven you could leev zo much bedder und no vork at all."

Mrs. Ames, whose fine eyes had been intent on divining his meaning, said: "I can do very well without work from your house or advice from you, sir. I will finish this piece, but will never do another stitch of work for your firm, and you can go immediately," pointing to the door. "God will care for me and mine, and in Him will I trust. Not another word, but go!" she exclaimed in decisive tones as she saw that Mr. Sneekinswine was again about to open his mouth.

As he stood with his hat in his hand there was something in his manner so odious, so repulsive and insolently overbearing, that Jean, who was too young to understand the import of his broken English, was so enraged, and knowing that it must mean something terrible or her mother would not have spoken to him thus, stepped at once to the door and opened it wide that he might pass out as quickly as possible.

To add injury to insult, the great, coarse, vulgar-eyed sensualist, stepping in front of Jean, said:

"Vot a buffictly boochiful girl Mees Ames eze. Of she vos mine little girl I vud but her in von glass caze only to be looked at; she should not vork;" and with an attempt at a bow, he passed out.

Jean was not long in giving the door a bang behind him.

"No one will ever say he is 'buffictly beautiful,'" Jean sneered, as she jerked up the chair whereon the wretch had only for a moment sat.

Mrs. Ames, divining her meaning, cried:

"Why, Jean, the man did not sit down at all."

"O, yes, he did, mother," and she carried the chair to the woodshed, where old rubbish and odds and ends were stored, and threw it on to the heap as she would have done such human rubbish as Mr. Sneekinswine.

Mrs. Ames would have been overwhelmed at this episode had it occurred the week before, but to-day she scarcely gave the creature a passing thought of contempt, so supremely occupied was she with what Mr. Murdstone would be like, what he would say to her, and how the interview would likely terminate. But this little scene had much to do in riveting her resolves to listen favorably to Mr. Murdstone's proposal.

CHAPTER VI.

THE MARRIAGE.

One night, soon after this little event, as Jean came home from school with her books on her arm, her bonnet half falling off, her hair in great, loose, tumbled curls in wild confusion over her neck and shoulders (she had romped hard as well as studied hard that day), she saw, as she neared the house, a gentleman sitting just inside the door, so tall that there was no room for her to pass, so she went around to the back entrance, piled up her books, brushed her hair into a little less confusion, but took small time; for since the unpleasant visit of the man the week before, Jean was very suspicious. When she entered, she saw in a moment that her mother was looking very bright, and much happier than usual; that the gentleman's face, too, was lighted up, though he had on every-day working-clothes, coarse boots, and flour all over his coat and pants in spots that looked like "patches of snow in December," giving him a very rugged, picturesque look. He had a modest, retired, something of a gentlemanly air about him, and seemed conversing in an easy, friendly manner with her mother; at least Jean thought he seemed friendly.

He scarcely looked at Jean when her mother said: "This is my daughter, Mr. Murdstone," but went on talking about Jean's father, whom he had often heard preach, and greatly admired, and soon afterwards took his leave, saying he would call the following Sunday.

Jean jumped up and ran to her mother as soon as he was out of the house, crying, "Oh, mamma, what does he mean by coming next Sunday? Nobody wants

"I can't have him for my father," sobbed Jean.

to see him; why didn't you tell him, mother? What is his business?"

Mrs. Ames, with great candor, answered: "Why, my dear child, he wants to marry us, and take us all out to his farm in the country."

"And cover us all over with flour?" cried Jean, "Marry us! he'll not marry me," she continued with a sneer, and sat down on a chair against the wall and burst out crying.

"Why, my dear child," Jean's mother replied, soothingly, "Mr. Murdstone has four little girls, all smaller than you, that you can have for sisters."

"I don't like Mr. Murdstone, and I can't have him for my father," sobbed Jean.

"Why, Jean, I am astonished at you. Mr. Murdstone may fall off his sacks of flour as he goes home to-night, and never be thought of again."

"Oh, if it could be so," moaned Jean.

Mrs. Ames did not like to hear her child protest so bitterly against this marriage. She was not superstitious, but she did believe the sensitive soul stands bare, sometimes, quivering against the cruelties of fate. Was it possible that this step, taken only for her children's good, might prove their greatest evil? For a moment her eyes took on that far-away look, and a cold shudder passed over her frame. In spite of herself, she felt the great faith that she had in Mr. Murdstone an hour before was shaken.

Jean remembered the bright look on her mother's face when she first came home from school, and now saw her looking sad. She was ashamed, ran away and washed her face, brushed her hair, and, coming back, said:

"Forgive your naughty child, mamma; but I did feel so bad a moment ago," and then the tears gleamed in her eyes again, and to hide them she ran and brought some wood, made a bright, blazing fire, and tried to think of everything for the evening meal; hurried hither and thither to do this and that, determined to put the hateful reality out of her mind. Then she brushed Alfred's hair, put on a clean apron, kissed him, and said he was the sweetest little brother a little girl ever had, and Alfred repeated all her words over again in his childish prattle.

This marriage was much more terrible in its consequences in wrecking Jean's happiness than that of her mother's, as we shall be able to prove as we proceed, and right here let the metaphysician tell us if it is possible that the "angel of the Lord" showed this to Jean and not to her mother, as of old he appeared to Balaam's ass but not to Balaam.

Mr. Murdstone, as he wended his way to the mill, pondered on what he should do. He liked the fine face of the young widow. She looked strong, almost robust when compared with the pale face of the little wife he had so recently laid under the sod, which was a strong point in the widow's favor. No man who has had one sickly wife wants another, no matter if it was his own cruelty that made her so; and summing up expenses, he said to himself: "The young girl might want to stay in town and continue at school, and then there would be but the two youngest boys. A few hard whippings, and the oldest one would run away, and as the baby looks delicate he may die. In that case, I should have the widow unencumbered. Why, here I am at the mill!" Mr. Murdstone's mind and legs had been making rapid strides and reached their journey's end about the same time.

Mrs. Ames had much better have gone on with her sewing, and done by Mr. Sneekinswine as Ellen Douglas did by James Fitz-James, who "knew every wily train a lady's fickle heart to gain, but here he knew and felt them vain." If she could have understood Mr. Murdstone's meaning as she did Mr. Sneekinswine's, she would have sent him about his business quite as rapidly as she did that gentleman.

We will let every one decide for himself which was the greatest rascal of the two. The one spoke his villainy right out, and she could defend herself and her little ones from it. But the other was subtler in his meaning, and came cloaked about in the garb of religion and morality. Think of a man coolly planning cruelty to the children of his beloved pastor, who had gone before and gained the eternal heights of glory that he himself was clambering for every day and hoping to gain. Just imagine a man planning to take a mother from her children, leaving them, without the slightest consideration, out in the world, deprived of a mother's care, her love, her tenderness all diverted from her children to his; not that he wanted his children to have any special, tender care, but that he thought a bonded slave by the marriage contract would be cheaper than hired help. He would just as coolly turn Mrs. Ames's children out in the world, and deprive them of her care, as he would fling the weeds that he had pulled out of his corn-field, over the fence into the road, and never give them another thought.

Mr. Murdstone, according to promise, appeared promptly on the next Sunday afternoon. Jean was at Sunday-school with her brother Will. He found only little Alfred at home with his mother. This fact of itself was sufficient to put Mr. Murdstone in great good humor with himself, and the thought was father to the wish that even Alfred might soon be out of the way. There were more than the average amount of subjects to be talked over before the preliminaries of a marriage that united twelve people instead of two could be satisfactorily adjusted by the high contracting parties, to say nothing of the little objecting parties. Mrs. Ames showed by her constant, motherly solicitude that she took *his* children right into her heart, and would care for and shield them from every harm just as she did her own. For this very reason, Mr. Murdstone found it rather difficult to propose to Mrs. Ames that she leave her children around hither and yon, among strangers, and the gentleman did not even make the proposition that he had thought out so boldly, of leaving Jean at school; and when Mrs. Ames frankly told him she would never think of taking this step, only to gain a sober, steady, industrious husband, who would be a good father to her children, Mr. Murdstone thought, "I cannot adjust these matters in regard to the children before my marriage." But, however reticent he was before, Mrs. Ames found him outspoken enough, immediately after the ceremony had been pronounced.

Mrs. Ames often thought that it was so strange that she had not noticed, before her marriage, that it was an alarming peculiarity that Mr. Murdstone had never showed any solicitude about her being good to his children, but it was she who had to ask if her children would be equally fed and clothed, and the same time allowed them for their education, and she remembered now, with pain, that he had hesitated as if it were a new idea to him, as indeed it was. Mr. Murdstone had been thinking how he would avoid doing all this, and not at all how well he would act the part of a father towards these children. He could no more be a kind father to his own children than a hitching-post could be the graceful bough of a weeping-willow tree. He was so cold, so sordidly mean and selfishly cruel, that he would not permit himself to be comfortable, much less allow children to be comfortable and happy. He was simply an old tyrant, inventing tortures for ten little children; and just as busy moaning and beseeching the Great Giver of all good to keep him out of hell. He never once dreamed of praying to be kept from doing a mean act so that he would not deserve the tortures of hell. The burden of his whole plea was: "God save me at last; don't punish me; don't sift my conduct; but take me straight to heaven without asking any questions."

CHAPTER VII.

THE DINNER PARTY.

Lest some tender soul should grieve for the fate of Mrs. Smith, with her six small children, mentioned before, we will tell them of the way Mrs. Ames provided for their welfare in the few intervening days before her marriage. She called on Mrs. Judge Seaton first. The Judge beamed a good morning upon her, as he stood in the hall, hat in hand, ready to go to his office.

"I am so glad to see you, Judge; I did not expect to, for I thought you would be gone to your office. You do look splendid in that last suit I made for you." It was a drab-colored broadcloth.

The Judge, glancing at his legs and then at his arms, replied: "It is comfortable—very."

"I'm glad to hear it," returned Mrs. Ames, "for it does not prevent you from expounding the law with great ease and composure." Just then a musical voice was heard on the stairway, calling:

"Oh, Mrs. Ames, do come right up; we've heard something about you. Dear old Dr. Knight was here last evening. I am so glad for you," continued Mrs. Seaton, kissing her rapturously. "You look as good as a ripe peach this morning, and I hope your intended is as grand a man as the world ever produced. He ought to be, I am sure. The Judge says he knows him quite well, and he is a good straightforward man in business; a little awkward and peculiar, perhaps, but all great men have their oddities. I know you have come to ask me to be your bridesmaid, but I have nothing to wear but my pearl-gray silk, and in that I should outshine the bride, and that would not do at all."

"Oh, you would outshine the bride in anything you might wear, Mrs. Seaton," returned Mrs. Ames, "so I shall dispense with a bridesmaid altogether;" adding, "You have not guessed my errand, and never could, so I'll just tell you what it is. I am so glad that Dr. Knight has already disclosed my secret to you." And then Mrs. Ames went on to give an account of Mr. Sneekinswine's visit, and Mrs. Seaton's eyes snapped, and she looked like a general riding to victory on a field of battle as she said:

"All the work of my household shall go to Mrs. Smith after this, and I declare, my boys do wear out their clothes so fast that sewing for them alone will almost support Mrs. Smith."

The two ladies talked for an hour, and planned for a basket dinner, to be given at Mrs. Smith's on the next Tuesday evening, when all of the people for whom Mrs. Ames had been sewing for the past two years should be especially invited to come.

As there were few people in that town who had the audacity to attempt to get into the world or out of it without the assistance of dear old Dr. Knight, so there was not a woman in the town who had the bravery to get up a party, or arrange any little benevolent scheme, without the encouragement of this worthy gentleman. They could come to no definite plans without first seeing him. Mrs. Ames called on the doctor as she went home, but he was ten miles out in the country, and his wife was not sure that he would be at home that night. She left word with this cheery, busy wife for the doctor to come, the next afternoon, to her house, or as soon as he could. The doctor's wife said that she knew he would be glad to enter into any plan by which Mrs. Smith would be assisted in making a living for her little children, and that Mrs. Ames could depend upon his calling at his earliest convenience.

Mrs. Ames, bidding Mrs. Knight good-bye, went

straight home to find Mr. Boggs, from the country awaiting her. Mr. Boggs was a brawny Scotchman with a broad brogue. He said his son James was going to be married this day two weeks, and insisted upon Mrs. Ames making his wedding suit. The cloth was a blue tweed, and Mrs. Ames was greatly tempted by the fine goods to do the sewing. Then she told the story of Mrs. Smith and her six children.

The honest old Scotchman wiped a tear from his eye, but said to Mrs. Ames, "Tha puir bie ha set his heart on'at to hav you mak tha suit, and he's such a hondsome bie, it 'twa be a pity ta disappoint him, and the bonnie lass as is gang to ba his woif is as particular as can ba."

At last, Mrs. Ames promised to make the suit if Mr. Boggs would agree to have all the work from his neighborhood sent to Mrs. Smith in the future.

"Upon ma woord, Mrs. Ames, it twa do ma sool good ta help tha puir widow," cheerfully remarked old Mr. Boggs.

The next day Dr. Knight came, according to request, and was greatly surprised to find Mrs. Ames busy again with her needle. She laughingly looked into his kind but surprised eyes, saying:

"Doctor, I think I'll give up that foolish idea, and go on with my sewing."

The doctor heaved a long, deep sigh, and looking up at the ceiling, said: "I am not sure but it would be the best thing; not sure."

Mrs. Ames dropped her needle and her work slid out of her lap. "Why, doctor, you alarm me."

The old doctor, looking at her with all the tenderness of a father, continued: "Was there ever wisdom enough in this world to enable anybody to know beforehand whether or not a marriage would be a happy one? To all appearances, as far as I can divine or look into futurity, yours promises to be the right step for both parties. Men want to be good and they want to be happy, but they don't know how to take care of their wives. There is not one man in a thousand that is fit to take charge of the happiness of a woman, and yet women trust them implicitly. But, my dear, what did you want to talk to me about this afternoon—surely not about weddings and such silly things?"

Then Mrs. Ames swallowed a sob that was about to choke her, and said: "Why, its something about planning this basket dinner for Mrs. Smith."

"Well, now, my dear, don't you know that not many of these fastidious, dainty creatures would go near Mrs. Smith, not even if they were invited to a funeral, much less an entertainment to prevent any number of funerals."

Mrs. Ames was again startled, thinking the doctor was going to throw cold water on her proposed marriage, and was also opposed to giving aid to Mrs. Smith. What had come over the doctor? She looked up with astonishment and asked: "Doctor, what do you mean?" But the doctor, who knew the exact social status of every mortal in the whole county, coolly replied: "My dear, send out your invitations for the ladies all to meet here at your house, with their baskets overloaded with good things; they'll everyone feel flattered, and such basting and brewing, such mincing and stewing as you'll set going hasn't been done in the last year. You get them all here, and I'll make a little speech explaining everything, and put them all in a good humor, notwithstanding their disappointment, if I can, and will head the procession over to Mrs. Smith's. The poor thing is about prostrate with grief, since she has lost her employment at the firm of Sneekinswine & Brassfielder. She sewed for them for so many years, and has not the least bit of faith in being able to secure for herself custom-work directly from the people. Poor woman! there is some excuse for her. I don't know what I should do if I were thrown out of my practice and compelled to go into a drug-store. I would feel lost, and would scarcely know where to begin. Old Badger and I have tramped day and night over the prairies, into town and out of town, and we shouldn't either of us know what to do if we didn't keep jog, jogging along;" and pulling on his gloves, he said: "This won't do. I've at least three more patients to see to-night. Badger's hungry and tired, and ought to be put into the stable to feed and rest. 'The merciful man is merciful to his beast.' I will call in the morning and take some of your invitations, if you will have them ready, Mrs. Ames, and hand them to the parties myself. Whatever aid I can give, you can depend upon." So saying, he stepped into his buggy, and old Badger went jogging along. The days passed quickly by and the evening came, and with it the ladies, their baskets brimful, carried by grumbling husbands, smiling lovers, expectant brothers, and one or two charmingly brave old maids trudging along with their heavy loads.

Jean, who had been sent by her mother to hint to Mrs. Smith to get into her best dress, said, in her sweetest accents: "Mrs. Smith, put on your best dress and brush up your hair. Mamma and Dr. Knight are coming."

But Mrs. Smith, being wholly unused to pleasant surprises, protested, and looking in her very worst plight, answered:

"I will do nothing of the kind. The doctor has seen me in my worst dress many and many a time."

Just then the door opened, and there stood the doctor, Jean's mother, and about twenty others, and unceremoniously all tramped into the little room, which was already quite full of children, there being three or four of the neighbors' children together with the six little Smiths; but Dr. Knight, who was in a dilemma every day of his life, and had his wits sharpened thereby, was ready for emergencies.

"Open the dining-room door, and the kitchen, too, Mrs. Smith, for we've all come to pay you a visit, and have a good time. Right this way, gentlemen; I've been here before, you see."

And soon the baskets were emptied of their contents, and such a sumptuous feast was rarely ever spread at any gathering that that town had seen in many a day. There were roast turkeys and baked chickens, ham sandwiches, tongue sandwiches, and a whole roast pig, with a corn nubbin in his mouth, which made all the children clap their hands in fun to see. There were boiled hams; there were tarts and pies and jams, jellies and canned fruits; and there were cheese and pickles, and such heaps of bread, and such rolls of fresh butter, and such piles of great, snowy cake, to say nothing of the cookies and gingersnaps and gingercracks and candies.

They soon all fell to, and the noise and laughter and merriment, eating and drinking, and general good humor, was heightened by the oddity of the whole scene; and the funny jokes that went round. No one knew what it all meant, excepting the old doctor, Mrs. Ames and Mrs. Judge Seaton, and they did not tell until a late hour. As each and everyone was acknowledging to Mrs. Smith that they never had enjoyed themselves so much any evening in their whole lives as they had that evening, the old doctor said he wished to extract, not their teeth, but a promise from them all that they would bring all the sewing that they had brought to Mrs. Ames to Mrs. Smith henceforth and forever, or as long as they required raiment, since none of them knew better than he, and his voice grew sad as he said it, "there comes a time to us all when we are no more in need of clothes, no more in need of human help; then let us be as kind to each other as we can while we may," and they were all glad to promise. Mrs. Smith, with a more radiant smile than anybody remembered ever to have seen on her face before, said she thanked them everyone from the bottom of her heart, and tears were just on the verge of coming, when her little five-year-

THE DINNER PARTY. 47

old Ted jumped like a squirrel upon the table spread over with good things, and glancing quickly at the table, then at the people, with hands spread like an eagle's wings, said: "I thank you all," and with a bound like a dart jumped to the floor and hid under the table. This electrified the whole company; their uproarious laughter was something to be remembered.

One burst of merriment, and Mrs. Smith was alone with her children and the loaded tables, for she declared she could not see that a mouse had nibbled off the feast, and many of the good things lasted her and the children a whole month. She also discovered two big hams and a side of bacon nicely sewed up in cloths, uncooked, but garnished with parsley leaves, and exclaimed to the children: "Dear Doctor Knight has done this—dear, kind-hearted old soul."

Next morning, Yates, the big-hearted baker, came with his bread-wagon, and said:

"Halloa there, Mrs. Smith; I see by the party you had last night you hav too much brod for you and de shildren to eat up in von month, so I tot, if you vil allow me, I'll shust tak von basketful and sell it to my gustomers and next veek I vill bring you some more vat is vresh again."

And Mrs. Smith replied, "That is a good idea, and you're very obliging, indeed. It looks now as if myself and children could hardly starve in this town, Mr. Yates."

"I should tink not, in this corn and hog country," said the baker, and his face shone like a bake-oven all in a glow, as he clambered into his wagon and drove away.

CHAPTER VIII.

PARENTAL AUTHORITY.

Mrs. Murdstone had been married a month. It was Sunday evening; the boys, Ben and Thomas Ames, had come out to spend the day with their mother, and see Jean, who was getting to be quite a tall girl, have a romp with their younger brothers, and get acquainted with their new step-brother, a quiet blond boy of the same age as Thomas Ames. When the two boys were together the contrast was so great, that no one could help noticing it.

Thomas Ames was a brown-haired boy, with dark keen eyes, that met your own with a pleased gracious expression, one that spoke as plain as words: "All the best there is in me is at your command. I wish to please you, and expect you to be pleased with me. Nothing can hinder my walking the earth a buoyant, expectant lad. There is a wealth of goodness, and possible greatness in me, and I have no need of curbing any of my best endeavors to please."

Dan Murdstone was quite as handsome a boy, with fine blue eyes. He was quiet and shy. Every act was constrained and hesitating, which made him awkward in the extreme. He did not dare to speak above a whisper even when the boys were at play among themselves, and on no account would ever speak in the house to anyone, and if spoken to would answer only in monosyllables. He was not a modest, sensitive, retiring boy, not that at all, but a stolid, alert, watchful spirit, determined not to be surprised by the enemy, who would promptly forbid any boyish sports, or still worse, wreak dire punishment upon him. A day spent with this boy, the only son of Mr. Murdstone, was enough for **Ben and Thomas Ames**; they had no notion of submitting **to tyranny that would** make **them** into such **boys as Dan** Murdstone appeared **to them to be. Ben had** just been saying to his mother: **"We have made up** our minds that **we can never come to live at Hickory Hall,"** and **he held** her in a **long and tender embrace, saying: "For** your sake, dear mother, **I would come,** but it would not help matters, not a bit."

He was **as** tall as she **now** and grown **quite manly. "No,"** she whispered, **"you are** right my **son; there are enough** of us here now, quite **enough,"** she added **loud enough** for Mr. Murdstone **to hear the** last words, **knowing this** would accord with **his feelings.**

Thomas was kissing his **new sisters all a** good-by **that made more merriment than was usual in** that **house. A cloud was gathering on Mr. Murdstone's face** that **made Dan tremble with fear; but Master Thomas, all unmindful of** terror, **never stopped till every girl in the house** had been given **a rapturous** good-by, **and walking up to** his step-father **reached his** hand in **his gallant fashion, and with** great deference **bade** his **towering step-father good-night; said he** had **had a** fine **visit at the hall, and** hoped **it would** be **his good fortune to visit** it often, adding a request that his **new brother might** spend **a** day with him in town. **Mr. Murdstone** was **pleased with the** deference the **boy** showed him, but **he acknowledged** it by **no token or** sign. **The boys took his hand and let go. It fell** listlessly **at** his side. **Master Thomas bowed to his mother a** little coldly, she thought, **the boys jumped into the buggy and** drove **rapidly away. That was the only day the whole** ten **children ever spent together; and they ever held it** in **remembrance.**

After the boys had driven out **of** sight **of Hickory Hall, Thomas** said: **"Ben, do stop** driving **so fast, I want to talk."**

"Well, I don't want to say a **word,"** replied Ben, **pulling** up the reins.

Then Thomas asked Ben: **"How could you stop to**

4

kiss mother good-by. If I had, I should have turned and clutched old Murdstone's throat. I could not have helped it. Did you ever see such a suppressed boy in your life as Dan Murdstone is? That boy has been beat every day of his life, and I should think twenty times a day by the way he acts." Ben answered:

"Why did I not go and see old Murdstone and his children before mother married him? I was a boy, and could not think of interfering in such matters," he said, as if talking to himself, "but I'm a man now. I believe my hair has turned gray to-day," and he took his hat off and pulled his brown curls.

"Well," said Thomas, "I don't feel so bad about it for mother, as I do for his own children. But wont he have a merry time whipping those children with mother in the house? She won't christianize him; oh, no. He's already a Christian. Did you ever hear such a long blessing given at the table, Ben? She'll humanize him, mother will."

"Well," said Ben, "what a philosopher you are. Humanize him, indeed. It would take a far longer and harder tussle to humanize him than the wildest gorilla that ever was caught in South America. Just imagine his long arms swinging a whip over a boy's back. Do you wonder that poor Dan lives in perpetual terror? You wouldn't think him so easy to humanize if you had seen his face grow black, as I did, when you were raising that rumpus, kissing the girls good-by." "That little child, Nell," said Tom, "is the prettiest child I ever saw; sweet as a rosebud, and a gentle and affectionate little creature, too, and they all love our mother as much as we do."

Ben was older than Thomas, and felt that he was in some sense responsible for his mother's happiness. His young blood made him restive. How was he to live and know that his mother, his sister Jean, and his younger brothers were daily subject to cruelty, his lovely, cultured mother doing all the menial labor for all that big family. Ben grew savage, took the whip from its socket, and struck the horse a fierce blow that made him rear and plunge, and finally run until he had all he could do to hold him.

That night he moaned out a prayer, and awoke next morning with a headache. He said to himself. "I must stop thinking of old Murdstone, or I shall be a lunatic in less than a week."

If the boys could have looked back over that long stretch of road, through the waving corn-fields, and past the bending orchards, that night as they were driving home, this is what they would have seen:

Little Alfred in his mother's arms, he being fretful and she wearied with the cares of the day. She stepped to a fence near by, which separated the door-yard from the corn-field, and seated Alfred on the top rail under the leafy canopy of a peach-tree bough that was loaded with forbidden fruit—Mr. Murdstone having told the family not to pick those peaches. This amused the child for a moment, when, with a scream of delight he reached his little hand and snatched a ripe peach that hung near his head.

Mrs. Murdstone saw her husband coming with rapid strides, and took the child in her arms, saying: "My precious child, how could I have put you up there?" He, without saying a word, jerked the child from its mother's clinging arms with a hard, cold, determined jerk that would have torn its little arm from its socket if the mother had not let go; then breaking a limb from the tree, he whipped the little three-year-old child unmercifully. The poor little fellow, who never was struck before in his life, was frightened almost to death. Jean, the dauntless Jean, ran to her brother, took him in her arms and tried to soothe him, but, as soon as he could speak for the pain and choking and strangling and crying, he cried out, like one making a terrible struggle for help, "Mamma, oh, mamma!"

That cry went to his mother's heart. She was trembling like a leaf, but did not dare to reach her hand to her poor, bruised, defenseless child, but her heart could and did go out in a great silent cry to God for mercy. Jean was outraged at what seemed to her like cowardice in her mother, but which was really schooled wisdom, and she took her little brother and let him slide into his mother's lap. Then she confronted Murdstone, the first time any human being ever had, and it was a new experience to that gentleman. She said, with defiance blazing in her eyes: "Don't you ever strike my brother again. If you must beat little children, beat your own, and let their mother in heaven look down on the cruelty, and stay God's vengeance from your head, if she can."

No words the child could have spoken could have affected Mr. Murdstone as these did. He was white as death. Jean knew by his prayers that he was a coward, and mistook his dyspepsia for religion; but in a moment, however, he rallied from his terror, and clutched a limb of that historic peach tree with such force that one-half of the tree with its weight of precious fruit, fell at his feet. It had been propped up on that side, having shown signs of weakness under its bending load, but prop and all now came to the ground. This mishap terrorized him still worse, for he thought he saw the vengeance of God at hand, but he was so used to whipping the children that nothing could deter him from his strong force of habit. He broke off quite a large, but now useless limb from the fallen trunk, and commenced wearing it out in a most vigorous manner over Jean's shoulders. Jean, instead of running to her mother, as he thought she would, stood like a heroine as she was, and took his blows, while he with his towering pride and rage, cowed under her words of contempt. "A noble father, beating a little girl! Oh, I shall respect you all my life for this," she hissed at him; "but you will never make me a poor, frightened, trembling thing like that," she said, pointing to Kate Murdstone, who had begged Jean not to say a word when her father was whipping little Alfred. Jean had pushed her off, saying: "Not if he kills me, will I keep still." The enraged brute, as intoxicated with anger as ever a man was with whisky, glanced at Kate as Jean pointed to her, and the poor girl, under that angry look, fell violently to weeping. This roused him still more, and he struck Jean one fearful blow that sent her reeling against her mother, and then flew at Kate with such vengeance that Mrs. Murdstone had to interfere. Putting her hand quietly on his arm, she said: "Father, father!"—with such a wail—"just stop, do, and think what you are doing." He did stop, but not until the girl's flesh was cruelly welted.

Just then, Dan, his eldest son, a boy of twelve, who had been to drive the cows home, had the misfortune to come at the wrong moment. He took in the situation quicker than a flash, and started to run. His running was a crime. Murdstone called him back. The boy had nothing on but a straw hat and thin shirt and pants. Every blow the father dealt made a welt as big as one's finger on the boy's tender flesh. It had been a hot day, and the boy had played harder that day with his new brothers than he was accustomed to do. He was looking for his mother to tell her how bad his head ached, when the brute he called father accosted him. The fear and anger together, so overcame the boy that he grew deathly sick. He sat down on the door-step and wailed:

"Oh, mother," and she was at his side in an instant.

The boy was white as death and limp as a rag. She looked beseechingly to Murdstone and said:

"He is dying."

He rallied soon, however, and vomited, and together they carried him into the house and laid him on her own bed. Everything was soon done that could be, but it was plain that he would have brain fever.

That night, Mr. Murdstone said the same long grace at supper. No one heard it but his wife. He took no notice of her wan face, nor asked why the children were not there. He knew they would rather go supperless to bed than see his face again that night. He wanted to rule, and he sat there in his princely authority—over the dishes—and wielded his knife and fork as though nothing had happened, and that night slept just as soundly as though he was monarch of a throne, had conquered an army, and hundreds lay weltering in their blood, while he was crowned with laurels of his own vain imaginings.

CHAPTER IX.

MURDSTONE'S REPENTANCE.

That night Mrs. Murdstone sat by the bedside of little Dan, who was quite delirious, throwing his arms about, muttering in his sleep, and writhing in pain. She put cold cloths on his head. There should have been hot cloths laid all along the spine. They would have relieved the nervous irritation. When the boy grew more quiet she knelt down and asked God for guidance in her great need. Once she thought she would call Danny's father, and crept timorously to his room. He was sleeping so soundly that he did not wake at her call, so she crept softly back to find Danny awake and in his right mind.

"Don't call him," he said, "he'll whip me to-morrow if you do."

"Oh, no, Danny, he wont ever whip you again. I have asked God to keep your father from getting angry at you. He will hear our prayer, my child, I know he will."

"My mother, oh, my mother," he sobbed. She stooped and kissed him, and held him to her breast until he was quieted. Then he said: "I am so glad my mother is dead. She was not like you. It broke her heart; it killed her. Do you think she sees you now so kind to me? Do you think she can see all the way from heaven?"

"Yes, my child," she answered, "she is right here to-night, helping me to nurse you."

"I don't know," he moaned, "she was afraid to do anything for me when she was alive."

"Well, I will lie down beside you, and perhaps we

can go to sleep," whispered Mrs. Murdstone, soothingly.

He tried to turn, but found racking pain in every muscle, and then asked: "Do you think there is a hell? He'll go there if there is. My mother always said he would, and I know he will, too."

Next morning Dan was in such a high fever that even Mr. Murdstone himself was alarmed, and sent for Dr. Knight. In a few hours the doctor was there, examined the boy's pulse, looked at his tongue, asked a great many questions, and shook his head mysteriously, saying:

"This is not like an ordinary fever case—tongue not coated. This is not bilious malaria. Murdstone, I think the boy will have to be bled, to relieve the congestion of the brain," he continued, pushing up Dan's sleeve for that purpose.

Mrs. Murdstone quickly but gently protested, feeling sure that the doctor would see the bruises on the boy's arm.

Murdstone, who had been standing by the bedside, suddenly thought of the doctor's horse, and went to put it in the barn. Dr. Knight was not going to allow his medical advice to be so easily set aside, so took the arm of the unconscious boy, and, turning up his sleeve deliberately, there to his horror found the great welts and bruises, and exclaimed:

"Why, Mrs. Murdstone, what is this?" Then she gave, through her tears, a short and wonderfully palliated description of the scene that had taken place the night before. The doctor, listening to the story, gently laid the bedclothes aside and examined the back and limbs of the suffering child.

"The only thing that can be done, Mrs. Murdstone, is to soothe these wounds with a dressing of sweet cream. Oh, yes, he will live; but it will be weeks before he will be out of this bed. It was the fright and the anger that affected his brain; so it will take much longer for the nerves to recover than the muscles," and

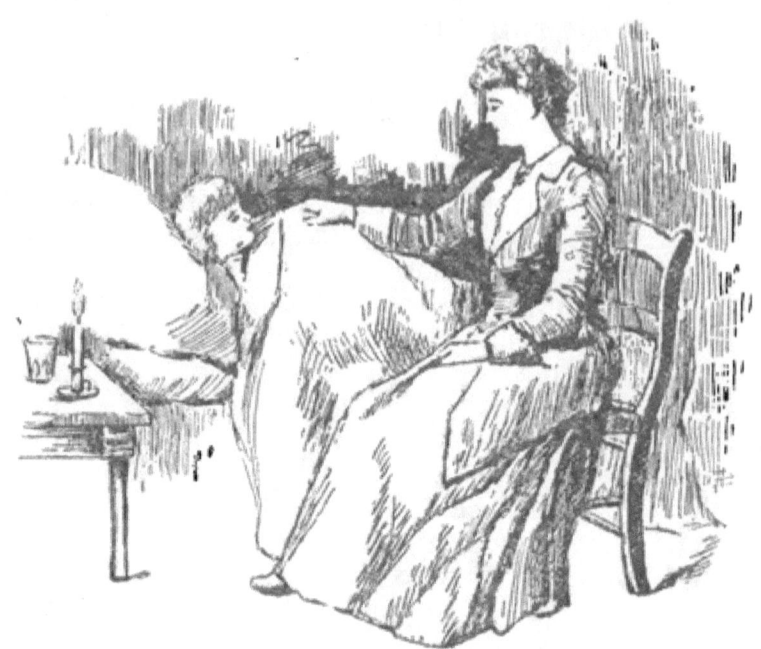

"Do you think she can see all the way from heaven?"

MURDSTONE'S REPENTANCE.

then he added to himself, "Murdstone ought to be dealt with in the church for this." Then to Mrs. Murdstone: "I will take Murdstone to town for some medicine for little Dan. I will give him a talking to, and see if he beats me too."

"Well," said Mrs. Murdstone, "Kate and Jean's arms and shoulders are just as badly bruised as the boys', but their dresses protected their limbs."

Dr. Knight looked at Mrs. Murdstone's wan face, and said: "Why, how can you endure this? I should think you would leave him; the man must be crazy."

"Leave him!" exclaimed Mrs. Murdstone, "and leave these poor motherless orphans; disgrace myself and little children? No; you don't know me, Doctor Knight. With God's help and yours, I hope to persuade Mr. Murdstone to control his terrible temper. That is the only remedy."

Dr. Knight staid, watching the boy's symptoms, until dinner was announced. As soon as the meal was over, the two men started on their long ride to town. Murdstone was attacked by one of his depressed states, bordering on the melancholy of insanity. The quick eye of the man of science saw this, and saw, too, that the man must be quietly managed, or the cruelty of words from him might be much greater to Mr. Murdstone than his blows had been to the sensitive nerves of Dan—with this difference, that the one man struck his blows in ignorance of the wrong he was doing, while he believed himself to be doing a duty. The doctor could not plead ignorance, and therefore had to be cautious and merciful as the gentle dew that falls from heaven when most needed, at the time when the fierce sun withers and scorches the tender plant.

The old doctor was a medium-sized, round, plump, man, who settled himself into the well-worn cushion of his old-fashioned gig in a most comfortable manner, and let old Badger jog along over the smooth road in the warm afternoon sunshine. Dr. Knight had intended giving Mr. Murdstone the hardest talking to he had ever given a man in his whole life, but one of his sighs, as he seated himself beside the doctor, together with his dejected look, caused him to change his mind and he pulled his hat over his eyes, gave Murdstone the reins, and in two minutes was taking a refreshing nap. Murdstone was restless, pulled old Badger this way and that, and finally got into a quarrel with the plodding, patient old horse, and reached over to get the whip. Old Doctor Knight was awake in a moment and arrested his hand, exclaiming:

"No, not for your life, Murdstone—don't do that!"

Then he took the lines and the whip to put it back in its socket, adding: "I never struck my horse nor my dog, my wife nor my children, in my life, and Murdstone, had I known that you did, I should as soon have asked Mrs. Ames to build a funeral pyre and burn herself alive as to have asked her to marry you."

The doctor wiped a tear away as he continued:

"You are dear to me as a brother, but I must tell you that I have not skill enough to save your son. If your wife's nursing and God's mercy will spare him he will live, but nothing I can do will save him. If you had been considerate and tender with him as a father ought, you would have seen this fever coming in the boy's languor, and by gentle sympathy have soothed his headache yesterday, instead of making him so much worse by giving him such a terrible whipping."

"Why, what am I to do," asked Murdstone; "have no authority in my own house?"

"Why, man alive, yes, all the authority in the world, but not that kind; such harsh, not to say cruel treatment of children, is not the kind to be given by the father of little children. It is all habit, Murdstone. Now, see me stop old Badger; a feather's weight on this line will stop him," and with the slightest touch, the horse stood still.

"Oh yes," said Murdstone, "that's very different.

He wanted to stop, but you just start him up and see if it don't take a little more force."

"Oh, no," said the old doctor, "If I just take the lines in the most quiet way, giving old Badger the slightest hint of my wish, he will jog on," and suiting the action to the word, sure enough, up trotted the old horse.

"Now, Murdstone, don't I exercise as much authority over my horse by these gentle means as I should if I used the greatest violence? It is just so with my children, and you can do the same, Murdstone, if I can."

"I used to whip the children too much, I think myself, when they were little," confessed Murdstone, "but I have not so much since their mother died, for they were her last words: 'Don't whip the children,' and they ring in my ears for days after I have whipped one of the children."

"I should think then you would be very careful how you ever let your temper get so much the better of you as to strike one of them," said the doctor firmly.

"Temper?" cried Murdstone.

"Yes," said the doctor, "temper and bad rearing. I would venture anything now, Murdstone, that you grew up under the most stringent, if not the most absolutely tyrannical domestic discipline. Is it not so?"

"Well," said Murdstone, "if to be boxed on the head by the great, heavy hands of my five old-maid sisters, until I went spinning to the other side of the room, about fifty times a day, was tyranny, then I had it. I believe it is the cause of these awful headaches I have so much now."

"It is very probable," replied the doctor. "To box a child on the head like that is a fruitful cause of deafness, and such treatment as you speak of would cause the death of any child in the world, if he had not that tough, muscular development that you are endowed with, my friend. One of your children would not live a week if they had to go through such an ordeal.

What were your parents thinking of to allow it, Murdstone?"

"My father died before I was born. My mother did often shield me from a hard knock, I tell you."

The doctor looked at Murdstone in pity, saying:

"What a spoiled childhood! How sorry I am for you. What a warped, hard, dwarfed life yours has been. I am sorry for you in my very heart."

"Is my child so sure to die, then, doctor?" said Murdstone. "And you think he would not, if I had not whipped him yesterday? God's hand is heavy upon me, surely. He is my only son. This is very hard, very hard, Dr. Knight," and he leaned back and groaned aloud.

The light was breaking in on the doctor. He was finding that Murdstone had really got a heart, and could grieve at the thought of doing a wrong to his child, but the man had such a hard, selfish nature that it took the fiercest affliction to thaw it out so that even the old doctor could discern the better part of the man.

"My friend," said the doctor, "I have never had such a wrenching since I commenced the practice of medicine. I would never see another case while I live if I had to encounter another like this, Murdstone—not if I knew it. I have been through many trying cases, that you know, but nothing like this, nothing."

"You have no hope, doctor," he said, again, "no hope?"

"What words?" repeated the doctor. "No hope that you will change into a reasonable, tender, kind, thoughtful father, as you ought to be—as you ought to have been yesterday, Murdstone? Your wife believes in your having the ability to control your temper; but I must confess I have no hope. The boy may live with her nursing, but, Murdstone, he had better die than live in perpetual fear of you. All the sweet, tender love of his young life turned into demoralizing fear and possible hatred of his father. No hope! Gods! to be a physician. Why I would rather be a hangman, and

MURDSTONE'S REPENTANCE.

done with it—a hangman, Murdstone. Why, that dead man whose children I thought you would be a father to, was my dearest friend. I loved him. Your wife is a pitying angel, I held in high esteem. Mrs. Murdstone, whom I have so basely wronged in that I asked her to listen to you kindly, is to me as a sweet sister, and you I have loved, Murdstone, and pitied. Oh, how I have and do pity you. Now, if your child dies, will you, Murdstone, see in its death God's chastening hand, and try to see the way to lead your children and not drive them? Tell me, Murdstone, will you, living or dying, try to *lead* your children to do right? And I will try to pluck up courage and go on with the case. God may spare his chastening rod in mercy this time."

Murdstone was bent under his great grief, his head almost down to his knees; the tears were blinding his eyes. They were at the drug-store as the horse stood still. Murdstone silently pressed the doctor's hand, and silently they got out, the doctor to compound the remedies required for the sick boy, and Murdstone to go to the church-yard, to the grave of his wife. There he knelt and took a vow never to strike his son again if God would hear only his prayer. He had not long to linger. There were no flowers on the poor, neglected grave. No flowers had bloomed for her in life. Why should they mock her in her peaceful grave? They did not. Murdstone picked up a little piece of the stone that had crumbled from that which marked her resting-place. This he hastily put into his pocket to remind him of his vow. The stone wore smooth with time, but not until it had worn many a hole through his pants that Mrs. Murdstone had mended many a time. She knew it meant something sacred to her husband, but never asked why he wore that precious stone.

CHAPTER X.

PREPARATIONS FOR CROSSING THE PLAINS.

Dan's recovery was very slow indeed; just as Dr. Knight had predicted. His new mother watched with him day and night, giving herself no rest, only at such intervals as the boy was sleeping peacefully. The next day, as the doctor was questioning Mrs. Murdstone about the symptoms of the boy's condition, he discovered there had been a complete change since the hour that Mr. Murdstone had knelt at the mother's grave.

The doctor's faith in the power of drugs had been greatly shaken many times of late, and his faith in prayer was increasing as the years, with their accumulating evidence, had brought fact after fact of this kind to his attention, and he confessed as much to Mrs. Murdstone. Dan's fear, trembling and nervous restlessness had all disappeared, but he was compelled to lie there, his prostrate vital powers at a very low ebb, for weeks. Who can count the result of that one hour's giving way to brutal anger, and cloaking the atrocity in the mild term of " parental authority?"

No sooner were the alarming symptoms of the boy somewhat relieved, than it was noticed that Kate Murdstone was moping in a listless, tired way, with such a quiet, spiritless, inattentive state of mind that it was positively painful to see her. She never recited a lesson in school, nor seemed to take the slightest interest in either play or study; her hands lay idly in her lap, or dangled heedlessly at her side. One evening, as the children were running, jumping and playing pranks as children do when dismissed from school, suddenly Kate reeled, stumbled, and would have fallen, but a strong boy, running back, saw her and caught her in his arms. She cried, "Oh, I am blind." Jean rushed to her side, saying: "Oh, no, it is the hot sun that has made you dizzy; lean on me."

Kate never spoke again. It took both Jean and the strong boy to carry her home. The next week they laid her beside her mother in the church-yard. The pure young maiden, the fair young girl, was at rest with her mother in heaven.

Dan was slowly recovering; all the fall and winter he could not take his place at work, only to do light chores about the house and grounds with his mother. He was never better pleased than when he could do something to lighten her labors. She was more than a mother to him, and he filled the aching void of her heart for her absent sons, so they were all in all to each other.

The harvest was over, the corn had been gathered, the cattle housed for the winter, the sheep and hogs fattened for the slaughter, the turkeys penned for Christmas, the spinning-wheels had been humming all the fall months, the heavy skein of woollen yarn had been spun and colored into rich browns, greens, deep blues and pale blues, all hung in the great loft ready for the loom. Two hundred yards were to be woven. Why so much for a family of eleven? There were only eleven, now. Why! were there to be no more falls with spinning wool and weaving yarn in them? I fear not, for this family. No more years of full-garnered sheaves o'erflowing with plenty—not here on the old homestead.

Oh, yes, more years in plenty, but hardships, struggles and scattering the young flock—the old story.

The old house had been sold. The family remained until the next fall, but commenced early to have the spinning and weaving done for the next year. Hence the preparations for the two hundred yards of cloth, which must be cut, fitted and made into garments.

Mrs. Murdstone was not a weaver. All the weaving was done at a little homespun factory just struggling into existence at that time. Much of the spinning was done by a hired girl, who was paid one dollar and a half a week. The girl was neat, tidy, and tired every day when the work was done; but she earned money, if ever so little; was independent and happy, and her wants were few. She was unlike some who worked harder and got no pay; who, after their marriage, were not independent, and too often wretchedly unhappy. But such was life in the Hoosier state, as I remember it, forty years ago.

The neighbors thought the Murdstone family, since they had united with the Yankee family of Ames, had gone daft. "They are anything but clear-headed. Going to cross the plains in ox-wagons to the Pacific coast! Of course, the Indians will kill them and take the wagons, horses and cattle before they get half way there. If the old fools wanted to go off by themselves, and be killed by the Indians, it would be all right, but to take all those helpless little children that don't even know what it means, is just awful, and the authorities ought to put a stop to the idea."

The scheme was so gigantic, the difficulties so terrifying, the preparations so all-absorbing, that it took nearly the whole neighborhood, busily working with might and main, to get the family ready at the end of the year, for the journey which would take a year to accomplish, even if it were successful.

"What if the Indians should take them all prisoners and make them work for them as slaves all their lives, and the journey never end? Oh, the horror!"

The neighbors sat around their firesides and talked "Indians" until they half expected the savages to enter with a whoop and yell, and, tomahawk in air, scalp them all in their peaceful homes. Then they would brace up at a corn-husking and say: "Oh, nonsense,

PREPARATIONS FOR CROSSING THE PLAINS. 65

Murdstone will never go, no more nor I shall; they are only talkin'."

"Yes, but see the way they are workin' like all persessed, the spinning-wheels just a-buzzing, and the looms a-whirring. Old Jake Cobe told me he had seventy-five yards of jeans to weave, some of it butternut colored, and some of it indigo blue, and old Mrs. Rogers were at our house last week, she were, and she sez Belling's man, what's the wheelwright in town, has got an order to put up two of the biggest kivered ox-wagons ever he seed in all his life; and they are to be made of the goldarndest tough hickory they kin git in the hull country—that sand wouldn't scrape, ner the sun warp, ner the water faze, to make it shrink er shrivel. You see there's hundreds an' hundreds o' miles o' nothing but sand deserts, and then there's nary a road the hull way, just brush and trees and sand and rivers to cross, an' savages don't make no bridges as ever I hearn on; they just stay on one side o' the river while the water is high and wait till its low. But you see, them Murdstones is a goin somers, God only knows where; they've jest got to push right ahead, cos' if they don't they'll never get across them biggest mountains in the hull world, just afore they get to that there awful fine valley, that I 'spose beats the land o' Canaan that Moses traveled forty years to see, with them children of Israel, and then only sot eyes on it and died. They say they are goin' for to take up land, and then they be agoin' to live and build up a country all by theirselves, with the savages just a-hootin' and yellin' and a-scalpin' of 'em all the time. Oh, yes, Davie, they are a-goin', or leastwise they be a-goin' to start, 'cos I never hearn o' Murdstone's not a doin' what he said he wus."

"That woman that Murdstone married is a mighty peert kind o' woman, and as good as wheat. The way she sot by them children o' his'n while they was sick with the fever this summer; and them children sets more store by her than mine does by me, a nuff sight, and she ses she can't tell no difference between which is her'n and which is his'n, only when they're sick, or be a-goin' to die, then natur' will tug away at her heart."

CHAPTER XI.

COMMENCING THE JOURNEY.

As there is an end to everything, so there was an end to the preparations, and a beginning to the journey.

On the morning of the twentieth of September, 1847, the ox-wagons, with their great, snowy covers, were standing in the yard, every inch of space packed with flour, bacon and beans, dried fruit, bedding, blankets, clothing and general camping outfit — everything in order. The wagons had been built for the trip; every convenience that could be thought of had been added for the comfort of the family. All the friends of the family, who felt the parting most keenly, had said their good-byes a week before — the good-byes never to be repeated. The curiosity of the passing friend and neighbor had been satisfied. Nurse Scott, who was going as far as the village with the family, was seated with all the little Murdstones in her ample lap, in the spacious carriage with its proud steeds impatient to be gone. If they could have known the weary miles they had to travel, would they, like many a poor mortal, have been so eager for the start?

The carriage moved leisurely down the lane, the dull-eyed oxen pulled slowly out, and the long journey was begun. The neighbors were somewhat saddened by this dropping out of a whole family from their midst, but they flung aside their stolid tears, and were soon dispersed, feeling half glad the journey was not theirs, as each took up his or her burden of life, lightened by the contrast of their own peaceful homes, and their paying avocations, to a long journey over an unknown region, with no home, no employment, no civilization but one to be hewed out of the eternal nothingness of a new world.

There were five yoke of oxen to each wagon. Mike Flannigan drove one of the slow-footed ox-teams hauling the ponderous load, with its creaking wheels slowly turning on their great iron axles, making a heavy doubt spring up in the mind of any one who knew how far those wheels were destined to roll, whether, at that pace, they would ever reach their destined goal or not. Mike's reason for braving the desperate foe, and leaving civilization behind him, was that he wanted more room to fling about his brogue, for "Begorra," said he, "that's all I have left me since Pete Mulligan married the widdy Daley." Any man who has never attempted to drive five yoke of oxen will have no idea of the undertaking, especially until these dull-brained animals get settled into the routine business of tramp, tramping, with the heavy, groaning load creeping after. There are always shirks in an ox-team, just as there are in the human bee-hive, and if the driver was not on the alert, two or three oxen would be left to pull the load; and with a journey like that, it would work disaster, for the cattle that pulled the load would soon be disabled, and as there were no recruiting hospitals on the route, every man and beast must be able to move on.

Mrs. Murdstone told her friends that with such a journey before her, there was no time for tears, and bade them all a cheerful good-by, stepping into the carriage; and poor, old nurse Scott's lap was left empty of the little Murdstones, and her heart quite disconsolate as she said they didn't care for her any longer.

The teams had about six miles to travel before reaching the village where Mrs. Murdstone had formerly lived, and from which town she was married two years before, and where Thomas and Ben Ames had been at work until now. The whole town turned out *en masse*, as they passed through the principal street. The horses were impatient, champing their bits, and could scarely be kept quiet during the hour while the handshaking went on, but the patient cattle stood still chewing their cuds, and some of them actually lay down in their yokes to rest, to the great amusement of the bystanders, with which the streets were thronged on either side. Many citizens expressed a desire to join the party, and wishing the Murdstones every success on their journey, hoping to hear a favorable report, declared that they would join them in the course of two or three years. Dr. Knight said it would not surprise him if half the town followed suit.

As everybody knows, it was only the next June, 1848, that the great gold discovery was made at Sutter's mill, California, and many a gawking boy who stood looking in open-mouthed wonder that afternoon at the Murdstone outfit, found himself in California before three years had passed, ransacking the mountains and hillsides, and turning the rivers upside down to get their gold, and some found the yellow metal in great abundance. But alas! too many found shattered lives and broken fortunes, and some found early graves, while others returned to the old civilization and settled down to their former avocations, their minds stored with wonderful knowledge of the great hegira to the Golden West.

That night, the Murdstones, one and all, declared they were glad to be in a strange country where no one could say good-by. The romance of their first camp-fire was something to be enjoyed; there they were under the great spreading oaks, just three miles from the village, the fire lighting up the grounds; the rustic table, set with a clean, white, homespun flax table-cloth; new, shining tin plates and tin cups for tea; the snowy bread and cakes, jellies, cold chicken, cold ham, pickles — was not that a picnic, a peaceful, restful time after the day's events? The children were tired of being cooped up all day in the carriage. The noise, the fun, the frolic around that old oak tree was good enough for them; the night was clear, with the stars shining overhead; the fire-light, with its fitful glare, threw a glamour about the whole scene that gave to the campers promise that the whole trip was to be one of pleasure.

The Murdstone family was stowed away in the two wagons, which, to their great surprise were almost as comfortable as two little bed-rooms, with many conveniences for toilet arrangements hid away in wall pockets fashioned in the wagon covers. The boys and hired men slept in a tent on the "ground floor" they said, declaring they had daisies and buttercups for carpets; but all they had to show for daisy carpets next morning, was one little, belated dandelion that had forgotten to bloom until all his neighbors had blown away in the soft down that the dandelion, in its old age, gives to the wind.

It is needless to say that these campers, one and all, slept soundly; no crying children disturbed the midnight air, no standing guard all night for fear of Indians. These people were in Illinois, six miles from the Indiana line; they had to traverse the two states of Illinois and Missouri before reaching the Missouri river, the starting-point, as it was then called, for the emigrants who were crossing the great plains.

The Murdstones started on the journey in the fall, and wintered in the city of St. Joseph, on the banks of the Missouri river, as many other emigrants did who started from the interior of the Western States to cross the plains. There were no railroads in those days, and it would be utterly impossible to make the journey in the early spring, as the ice, snow and slush made the roads impassable for heavy loads to join the company that was formed at this last point of civilization, to travel together in hundreds for mutual aid and protection against the savages through whose country they had to pass. It was not deemed safe to travel with less than one hundred and fifty armed men after leaving the Missouri river. Kansas and Nebraska were an uninhabited wilderness, over which roamed the buffalo and Sioux Indians.

Dear, old Doctor Knight had tried to reach the Murdstone camp early, and take the evening meal with the family, in the open air, under the grand old oak tree that had stood the storms of a hundred years, and spread out its smiling branches to as many summers.

"Doctor Knight, I've been in attendance with you, many and many a time. You can't hurry up a case of this kind. What's the use fussing? I never saw you so anxious to get away," said the nurse, Mrs. Chinks.

"No, I see," said the old doctor; "and since I am compelled to wait, Mrs. Chinks, give me a pen and ink and I will compose a letter which may compose me. A doctor's life is but a slave's at best."

Mrs. Chinks, laying the writing paper before the M. D., said:

"It's a lot of people you're always giving orders to, and keeping 'em jumping to do your dictation, and a king has seldom lived who has more people eager to do his slightest bidding."

"Well, well, Mrs. Chinks, I wish there was not any worse slavery in the whole world. I am quite content with myself now, thanks to you," and with his ear listening every moment, for a call from the nursery, he took up his pen and wrote rapidly:

"At CARGASWALAGENS, Midnight.

"*Dear Friends:* I am detained. I don't blame a child for not hurrying to be born to wear a name like that. It doesn't sound so awful as it seems when written. I was with you, in spirit, around the old oak tree last night. It is glorious to have the seclusion of one's own family. You must have enjoyed it to a degree, and were really better off without me; but I am so selfish, I wanted to have one more last time. You know we have had several last good-byes. Your start is made, and a very good one too, I think. You will have a joyous time right through this fall. The cattle travel so slowly that you cannot possibly be wearied with your six weeks' trip.

"The big family carriage, with its fine span of brood mares, drawing its precious freight, looked proud and defiant of failure. You are splendidly equipped, dear friends, for the journey. I did not think when you first talked of going, that such a magnificent outfit could be got together in the whole county. Why, it will inspire respect and admiration in the breast of every savage nation through whose country you pass. They will not harm a hair of your heads. They will be glad to see you, and learn some of your methods of life. They will not adopt them — civilization is not so easily reached — but the savages will be pleased and entertained, and will make no war upon you since you are only peacefully passing over their country. Do not allow the young men of your company to disturb their game too much; keep your guns and ammunition out of sight, but where they can be reached at a moment's warning.

"I shall miss you, but I am proud to have you there in that new world. I know your lives will be so much grander and broader than they could ever have been here. Why, you are establishing a new civilization. You will be so remote from other centers that it will be slow to build up a new state; but so much the more will your moral heroism be felt. Like primitive man, God's first temple, the trees, will be your houses of worship. But how soon will you build houses, churches and schools, and plant orchards. For the last two years I have been gathering choice varieties of fruits, flowers and garden seeds for you, and when they are all growing and blooming in splendor, then you will think of me. I know how readily you will lend a helping hand to the new world you are about to bless with your noble, strong lives.

"And the dear children — is there any four-walled country school-house in all christendom where they could learn as much as they will next summer, in the great world from which they will gather object-lessons as they pass on and on? Your girls will grace fairest homes, and your boys will sit in the legislative halls of a new state, and I shall probably read all this in the letters you send back, and how soon it will all come to pass, dear friends, and we shall be done with it all,

and like Jacob of old, be gathered to our fathers; and the old world where we have loved, lived and died, will move on just the same without us. I am called. Good-by."
  DR. KNIGHT.

CHAPTER XII.

CROSSING THE PLAINS.

Next morning, the family were at breakfast; the air being cooler, the children would have been uncomfortable but for this canvas house and the cooking-stove fire, with its beefsteak frying as homelike as you please, and the most fragrant coffee, with cream Mr. Murdstone had bought of a farmer who had allowed him the use of his barn-yard for the cattle, and stable-room for the horses, charging him but a trifling sum. There was, however, many another farmer on the route that took advantage of the situation, and charged him most exorbitant prices for the same accommodations. And while they were thus cosily and somewhat hastily swallowing the early meal, little Alfred, on his mother's knee, espied the letter that Dr. Knight had pinned on the tent door, where he had written in pencil, "Beware of midnight prowlers. Baby boy—mother doing well. 2:10 A. M. DR. KNIGHT AND OLD BADGER."

Mrs. Murdstone read the foregoing letter, and Thomas Ames, as he lifted the tin cup of coffee to the dawning down of his upper lip, exclaimed: "I will be the legislator!" and Jean said, "Read that again, mother. What kind of a home is it I'm to grace?"

"The Murdstones, as they wended their slow way along, could not have had a pleasanter journey. The road was good most of the way, and those glorious, bright days of autumn weather were just perfect in that mighty valley of the Mississippi. There were hundreds of miles of dead level,—not a ripple nor rise of ground,—one mighty sweep as far as the eye could reach in every way. The horizon sets down flat on the level plain. This vastness is sublime. It is awe-inspiring. It takes away your power to dwell upon little things like self. You wonder if this is eternity and there is no end, as day after day you go on and on, and meet only with endless expanse?

The people living along the route complained of being oppressed by this immensity of space, where there was nothing for the eye to rest upon, and they were glad when night shut in the earth with darkness; and yet, in the clear, bright moonlight, it was something weird and almost terrorizing to look upon. Mountain scenery is always soothing to the spirit of man. There are such sheltering nooks, such sublimity, such pure air, and yet, with all, such a protecting feeling. You flee to the mountains for safety or shelter; but where would you find shelter here if a storm should come, a wind drive you before it, or, as often did happen in those days, a devastating fire sweep over those prairies? No earthly thing could save you.

Our travelers had spent a busy winter in the city of St. Joseph, making the last preparations—the finishing touches, as it were—for the long journey across the plains. This was the last point of civilization through which they had to pass. Any supplies that were not laid in at this place would have to be done without; so the great throng that had spent the winter in that city had to have their wits about them, and decide what would be absolutely necessary, and omit what was not positively needed. A great many people took things they did not need, and found, after hauling them a few hundred miles, that it was necessary to throw them away to lighten their loads. The special family with which the reader is acquainted, were pretty level-headed, and did not make these mistakes. The wonderfulness of this lively little city of St. Josephs was that it sat on the rim of the world. You crossed the Missouri river and were out of the world and into a wilderness. It was wonderful, too, to stand on the banks of the river, and watch the palatial steamers as they plowed through the muddy water. How quickly the splash and whir and foam that they left in their track was smoothed away by the moving waters, and its bosom left unruffled by the slightest hint of any disturbance.

There are natures like this: Jean Ames was not unlike the great river in her calmness. Would the throes of grief disturb her breast, and the current of her life quickly close over it all, and smoothly glide on? We shall see. But first we must get our heroine, together with the hundreds and hundreds of her fellow-travelers, "the plains across." It would require the pen of a Dickens to describe the bustle and confusion; the noise, hurry and jostling; getting across the river, taking their places along the line, waiting to be numbered and put into position. There were about six hundred wagons that crossed the river in the first days of April, 1848. Each wagon was supposed to carry three adult people, with any number of children thrown in. Now this immense concourse of people had to be divided into companies, the first company to start out two days in advance, the next following in order, and so on. These companies consisted of one hundred and fifty wagons each. It happened that Mr. Murdstone was chosen as the man to lead the van, and as the horses walked faster than the cattle, they were allowed to go ahead. The gallant steeds looked defiant of failure, sure enough, though everybody was prognosticating their inability to stand the journey.

Captain Wambaugh, riding back and forth along the line of long teams, seemed proud as any general that ever directed a battle or led soldiers to victory. He was a French-Canadian, and understood the Indian character thoroughly. He was a well-knit, compact man of medium stature; a broad bronzed face lit up with clear, blue eyes, that meant to be obeyed without any palaver, and he was obeyed from first to last without anyone's feeling that he was under surveillance. These companies were to travel so as to be within hailing distance of each other; should a company be attacked by Indians, either at the front or rear; they could fall back or advance, as the case required. There were horsemen riding back and forth, so that each company had an account of the other's progress nearly every day. There were some rules to be observed, and one of them was, that the family that led the train one morning was to fall back to the rear the next. The teams of each family were allowed to remain together.

There were only two family carriages in the train—the Murdstones' and that of Dr. Martin's family. These were exempt from the rule of going to the rear, and were allowed to take the lead the whole journey through. Every night, when driving into camp, the wagons were placed in a circle so that they formed a compact corral, and as soon as the cattle were done feeding they were driven into this corral. A certain number of men were stationed at equal distances around the corral, to stand guard against the Indians until midnight, when they were relieved by the morning guardsmen. The hours after midnight were considered the most dangerous, as it is the Indian's character to creep up upon their foe just before daylight. Hence these were picked and tried men. Captain Wambaugh maintained a general supervision over all the companies, but a special one over the first company that led the van that year. He was chosen to this high trust because he had crossed the plains once before, and returned alone, braving every danger that his alertness could not dodge, which made him a hero with all the companies. Men were glad to trust someone who had had experience over these rough marches. It took stout hearts and strong hands to bid good-by to civilization, and move on with slow and steady tread to the goal of their destination—the sunset land of the Pacific ocean. Mothers folded their little children to their breasts and asked that God, who led Moses through the wilderness to the promised land, would care for their little ones. "Those were times that tried men's souls." There were roads to make, and bridges to build; there were trees to fell to make way through mountain gorges; there were swollen rivers to cross, made so by the melting snows, with only wagon-beds calked tight for ferry-boats; there were midnight vigils to keep, standing guard for Indians to shoot you if they chose; there were ravenous wolves, whose faintest howl would send the soul of a coward shivering to his boots. There were great bands of wild buffaloes, with frightened tread, thundering over the plains, making the earth tremble with their onward bounds. Horsemen must meet these frantic beasts, and turn them from their course, or they would sweep everything to destruction in their terrified way. There were hundreds of them, packed so closely together that each one must make his bound with precision or his fellow would trample him to death. Their fiery black eyes would look as if bursting from their sockets; their short horns almost bent to the earth; their great flowing manes glistening in the sun-light. If they were not warded off, they would crash right through the train, killing everything within their sweep. They were more to be dreaded than an Indian massacre.

There were mountain sides around which to clamber, where it was impossible to cut the solid rock and make a grade. Strong men would walk beside the wagons, holding them from falling off and tumbling down hundreds of feet into a torrent below. There were some mountains to climb so steep that teams had to be doubled to haul up one wagon. Then there were mountain sides to descend, when the cattle were taken away from the wagons, the tongue attached to the wagon, and large trees, with heavy tops, were cut down and fastened to the back for a weight to prevent their falling end over end, the places were so steep. There were other places over precipices where the wagons were let down with ropes. Then came the long marches over the burning sands, without water except that carried in casks, and sometimes the men, as well as the cattle, would give out on the long drives over alkali deserts. And here, as always, since the world began, the women came to the rescue when the men failed. There was one long march of three days that had to be driven over at night, as the heat of the sun was too intense in the day-time.

CHAPTER XIII.

CROSSING THE PLAINS.

The last night of this terrible tramp over the desert stretch Mr. Murdstone said to Jean: "There is no one to take the place to drive this carriage but you. There are so many men sick, and one poor fellow I fear will die before morning. The horses will keep the road. They will obey your lightest touch. All you have to do is to keep a tight rein when you go down the steep places." The brave girl did hold a tight rein down the steep places, trusting in God and the horses, and was wearied and worn with the marching when daylight dawned on the sand desert, and they were in sight of the winding river that lay a mile and a half below. The moment the almost famished cattle gained sight of the water they were unmanageable, and had to be unhitched from the wagons. They dashed pell-mell into the stream, which being shallow water saved them from drowning. There was a camp struck on the banks of Green river, and several days spent in recruiting the men and beasts from their never-to-be-forgotten all-night march.

The reader must not think that the whole journey was made up of such hardships as we have just described. There were weeks and weeks of very comfortable traveling, without anything occurring to disturb the even tenor of their way. There were miles and miles over the most beautiful undulating plains, covered with waving grass, and studded with gorgeous wild-flowers; over this delightful country they went creeping along at a very snail's pace. The cattle could not be made to travel more than ten or twelve miles a day, at the farthest, which gave the company ample time to enjoy the grand sights along the route. Away to the right and left there were snowy peaks crowning lofty mountain ranges, whose glowing tints in the warm afternoon sunlight were lovely to look upon; but resplendent, bathed in the glow of the setting sun, making the whole camp peacefully contented after the day's journey was ended; the cattle feeding leisurely on the vast plain; the camp-fires dying out; the evening meal over; men and women contented, happy and hopeful; children making the wild earth ring with their joyous merriment; young men and maidens acknowledging by their shy looks that "love rules the court, the camp, the grove"—all these, as they sat by the camp's dying embers, or wandered by the running stream's low banks, felt that the God who hewed out the mountains, set their snowy boundaries, sent the rivers singing through the valleys, and hung the sun, moon and stars over all, would shelter His children even in the wilderness, and this thought brought peace and rest and renewed strength, and thus they journeyed on and on, meeting new trials and new pleasures daily.

Hunting parties were often out by the dawn's early light, scouring the valley, the hill-top or mountain, just as it happened. Thus the company were rarely without the choicest game, elk, deer, mountain sheep; and the delicious antelope and buffalo, I fear, were killed too often, just for the mere sport, the men sometimes bringing in only the tongues, to show how many they had slaughtered of these fine animals, these monarchs of the plain.

Captain Wambaugh warned the company that they might get into difficulty with the Indians, if this wanton killing of the game was not stopped. On account of this, the whole train was compelled to halt one fine morning in June, and hold a pow-wow with the Sioux tribe of Indians. Some of the chiefs rode into camp and informed Captain Wambaugh that their people, who were just starting on a buffalo hunt to the south, would wait upon the company and receive what presents they had to offer for allowing the cattle to eat and tramp the grass; also for the game that the company were killing; a very honorable and praiseworthy proposition, and surely a company of the great American nation were not marauders, nor beggars; and so the captain said that the quicker the debt was paid, and with the greater show of generosity, the safer it would be for the scalps of the whole company; and the best policy for their pockets, as this tribe of well-dressed, well-fed and well-bred Indians, as Indians go, would not be outdone in generosity by the pale-faces, and the Indians, to make a display of their wealth, would present them with buffalo robes and dressed deer-skins, that might exceed in real value all the presents the Indians received from the company.

What the Indians most wanted was guns and ammunition, but that request could not be acceded to by the company. They would receive blankets, coffee, sugar, flour, tobacco. It was, therefore, arranged between Captain Wambaugh, and some of the lieutenants of the company, and the Indian chiefs, that the company should meet the Indians the next day, hold the pow-wow, and exchange the presents. Some of the horsemen of the company had ridden to the camp of the Indians, and finding that the Indian women and children were there, reported there was no danger, as Indians never go to war with their women and children.

Next day, everything being in readiness, the company drawn up in line, the wagons arranged to make as good a display as possible, the pale-faces with their best appearance stood in line, men shoulder to shoulder, their wives and children just back of them. The Indians were also arranged in the same order. There were three thousand of these Indians, who, if they had chosen, could have wiped the company of whites off the face of the earth in a moment, but they said they knew that the pale-faced nation was like the sand of the river bank, and to destroy this company would be to invite their own destruction; that they were friendly.

CROSSING THE PLAINS. 83

The pipe of peace was then passed from the Indian to the pale-face, back and forth along the line.

This ceremony ended, they all sat down upon the grass. Then the presents were brought and the exchanges made, and to the great relief of the company, they were allowed to move on to camp; and were glad to learn that they would meet no more Indians on the route until they had crossed the Rocky Mountains, as all their tribe had gone or were going south to lay in supplies for winter.

This tribe of Indians were stalwart men, straight as arrows; all dressed in their holiday attire of white buckskin, with long fringes, and deep-beaded embroidery wrought in a variety of colors and designs. The women were round and plump, some with oval faces and bright, sparkling eyes that were beautiful indeed. Their children were strong-limbed, fleet of foot and healthy as deer, and in point of physique would put to shame our proudest civilization.

Their children, under ten years of age, both boys and girls, wore no clothing, buckskin or any other kind of covering, but the skin that grew upon their bodies. There was not a sign of deformity or feebleness of mind or body. I fear not so much could have been said of the children of the company, who were more or less comfortably clad, but if they could have stood out, naked before scrutinizing eyes, as the little savages did, there would have been many a sunken chest, humped back and crooked limb, and traces of tears would have been found upon their countenances. As childhood should not be the weeping age, it would have looked bad for our civilization as we stood under the clear sky of that bright June day. A wild savage was never known to cut a stick and deliberately whip a child, hence they grow up without fear and without disease. Horned cattle never hook, nor kick nor hoof their young. The bible saying, "Spoil the rod and spare the child," if acted upon, would be the greatest boon that could be conferred upon humanity.

One of the leading savages, among the mighty chiefs

at the pow-wow, criticised the code of ethics of the company. The white children standing alongside their parents, peeped through the ranks across at the redskins who were standing about three rods away. The old chief's reprimand for this act of discourtesy was the chagrin of the proud American parent for many a day. After this grand pow-wow was over, the company passed a few straggling bands of Indians. Nothing compared to this grand Sioux nation, however, was again seen on the journey.

One bright day in June, just after the pow-wow with the Sioux Indians, there rode into camp six horsemen, armed and equipped for the journey with ample ammunition, guns, Colt's revolvers, bowie knives, and pack animals loaded with provisions. The train appeared something like the Queen of Sheba must have looked to Solomon, only there was no queen, and the camels were not bearing spices and jewels, but beans and bacon.

There was a king, however, but the boys called him Lord Cornwall. He was a young man, a little below the medium, with steel-blue eyes that went searching right through men, Indians, problems, anything. "A masterful man," one would say, as he stood by his horse that day, with his gun resting its stock on the ground, one hand firmly grasping the barrel, the other carelessly resting on the rein, together with a lock of the proud steed's mane; but ready, quick as thought, to mount, if occasion required. There was an alertness and bravery that shone from every movement and look, born of the necessity of looking out for danger. He and his men were twice taken prisoners by the Indians, and twice escaped, while crossing the plains on horseback, with pack animals, during the summer of '48.

Those who know him well, may recognize him as the president of the Mechanics' Fair; a man whose influence has been wide-felt in the marts of trade and commerce, and in helping to mold the country to its present greatness.

It had been a hot, long, dusty drive; man and beast were alike tired and glad of a rest in the cool evening on the banks of the bright, clear waters of North Bear river. The cattle had stood in the shallow stream, cooled their swollen, tired limbs, drank their fill of the pure mountain water, and now had to be driven out to get their feed of grass before dark. The grass was green on the banks of the river, and very tempting to the cattle, but the journey was telling on their tired and stiffened limbs, poor, dumb, brutes; many of them left their bones to bleach on the plains. They could not ask for liniment as the men did, but they could bathe their legs in the cool water, and did until they were driven out of the river.

It happened to be Mr. Murdstone's evening, with five other men, to drive the cattle to the best patches of grass; then as dark set in, to surround the whole herd and drive them all into the corral that was formed out of the wagons, for security against the surrounding savages. Mr. Murdstone had cut a long, thrifty, young willow to drive the cattle, at least so it seemed to Will Ames, a boy of eleven, whose duty it was to help drive the loose cattle behind the wagons during the day. Now the cattle were often tempted to run out of the road on either side to eat grass. It was an impossible thing to keep them in the road all day, especially as the train moved very slowly, often being interrupted and sometimes stopping for hours. The cattle had been restless with the heat of the day and roamed more than usual. The evening sun was setting, flinging a wealth of golden glory over mountain, sky and valley; the camp fires were smoldering. The young couples were wandering on the banks of the stream; children playing by the water's edge, throwing pebbles and wading. The old folks were lounging about the camp or sitting on the wagon tongues. All was peace and quiet.

Will Ames, fatigued with driving the cattle, was lying on the ground with his face to the sky, watching the clouds sailing along in the blue ether, tinted with that wondrous sunset glow, when his step-father came walking into camp with that long stick beside him, caught Will by the arm, saying:

"Sir, get up, and I'll settle with you for not keeping the cattle in the road, as I told you to do this morning."

Much frightened, the boy sprang to his feet, saying:

"I did, sir, try very hard, but the cattle would run out for grass."

"I'll teach you to obey me," and the long whip commenced to fall on the boy's shoulders.

Captain Wambaugh at that moment riding into camp, sprang from his horse, saying:

"Murdstone, hold, what are you doing?"

The two men glared into each other's eyes like madmen. The captain's hand was on his revolver in a moment.

Murdstone hissed:

"He must obey me!"

The captain—"You sir, must obey me!"

Murdstone, seeing the revolver, cooled rapidly, saying querulously:

"Am I to have no authority over my own household?"

"Authority? yes," answered the captain, "but while I am commander, an unborn babe's person shall be protected, or the person of a child but three days old shall be sacred. Don't I take every precaution to protect *your* person from the wild savages? And you, with your great strength, can strike a little child!"

CHAPTER XIV.

ARRIVING IN THE VALLEY.

It would be utterly impossible to give the details of the whole seven months' trip, as it would take the reader seven months to go over the ground with me, and I fear he would find it wearisome.

This company came tumbling down the Cascade Mountains into the Willamette Valley in the last days of October. The first thing they espied that gave token of civilization was an old worm fence, which was built pretty snug up against the foot of the mountain. The next thing that attracted their attention was curling smoke, which looked as if it issued from a chimney instead of from a camp-fire, flat on the ground. They turned a sharp corner of the road, and there was an old hen and her chickens—some dogs commenced to bark, and they were very near a log cabin by the side of the road. The company was rejoiced. People who have never taken so long a journey through an uninhabited region can never imagine the joy of these weary emigrants at the sight of the rudely-constructed human habitation. They bought some eggs, milk and vegetables, camped and were happy, notwithstanding they had still a long journey to make after touching this little hint of civilization. But they could buy grain for the cattle and vegetables for the camp. The company dispersed at this point, different families going in different directions, all vowing that they would soon meet again. They had spent many a pleasant hour planning how they would take up their land claims joining each other; how they would mark out desirable town-sites; how they would lay out these sites for prosperous cities. Some of the more ambitious ones declared they would send runners out to meet the emigrants the next year, and so get ahead of the neighbors in gathering a dense population about them; whereas, the truth is, that not a dozen of these families ever met again, and the realization of their dreams passed away like the smoke of the camp-fire, and most likely were never thought of again in the busy toil and stern necessity of the immediate labor of building homes for themselves and families. The moment these families were in the Cascade Range of mountains, and out of the range of the arrows of the redskins, they no longer remained together, but traveled just as they pleased, without any law or order. A few families that had formed friendships staid together, and assisted each other over the almost impassable roads. A few wagons had made the trip the year before and traced out a kind of road.

The storms, that winter, had felled many a giant fir across the almost obliterated track. The horsemen no longer remained to enliven the journey by their dash into camp with the fine, fat venison thrown astride their saddle in front of them; and all this made the last days of the journey toilsome and lonely enough. It is impossible to imagine how relieved those weary pilgrims were when the broad vista of the beautiful Willamette Valley first met their gaze; when they saw occasionally a little log hut, standing like a sentinel, giving promise of the future civilization of the Pacific Coast.

Mr. Barlow, an enterprising gentleman, one of the Hudson Bay Company's men, had pushed out to the uttermost confines of the new world; had built a log cabin and a few bridges across small streams as you come down from the western slope of the Cascade Mountains. At the last one he erected a gate through which everyone had to pass. This he called a toll-gate, which it proved to be, as everybody had to pay one dollar and a half per wagon to pass through, and in this way we knew the number of people who passed this gate, and Mr. Barlow reported that the whole six hundred wagons went through safe if not altogether sound. This report of itself was worth the expense, as it made everybody happy, and in after years they spoke with pride of the good management of Captain Wambaugh, and of the splendid health they enjoyed all the way, and with grateful hearts remembered how many dangers they had escaped. There were only three deaths reported in the whole company, but many poor cattle left their bones to bleach on the great sand desert.

The Murdstone family, in which I hope the reader has not lost interest, settled in the Willamette Valley, not far from where the capital of Oregon now stands. The Methodist missionaries, of whom there were about six or eight families, had settled at this point a few years before, and built a school for Indians on the site where the Willamette University now stands. They also put up a little saw-mill which had not sufficient water-power to run it except in the winter season. This place was called the Mission.

The Murdstones found a cabin shelter on a land claim, three miles outside of the Mission, where they wintered, as it was now in November, and too late to build a house; and strange as it may seem to the uninitiated, it was very difficult to find a desirable piece of land for a homestead; not but what there were thousands and thousands of acres of the best land that "ever crow flew over," as Mike Flannigan expressed it, that was well-watered and well-timbered. But this handful of emigrants, and a few of the Hudson Bay Company, together with the missionaries, had spread themselves over just as much territory as they could possibly take, so it required some time for Mr. Murdstone to look about and decide where he could wedge himself in, and Mrs. Murdstone said she really believed she had more comfort in the spacious old family carriage that the horses brought safely through. The children declared they did not want to live in a house; they very much preferred living out-doors, but when the rains came, with their patter on the roof, they were glad of a shelter, if only under the bare rafters. Around that kitchen table, lighted only by a tallow candle, many a well-thumbed book was read, many a hard sum ciphered, many a lesson conquered, that winter in that unpretentious cabin home. Mr. Murdstone took charge of the class in arithmetic and writing, for he was a suberb penman; Mrs. Murdstone of reading, history and geography. The older children attended the Mission School; the younger children had only the advantage of the evening school, as it was termed by the household. Evening prayers were said after the one tallow candle had been extinguished, for economy's sake, leaving only the bright blaze from the burning fir logs that were heaped up in a huge pile on the big stones that were laid on the hearth in place of andirons, and served the purpose well.

On the night of the twenty-ninth of November, when the rain had been falling in a soft mist all day, when one of the logs on the fire had burned down and fallen in two, making the hearthstone rather untidy, Mrs. Murdstone, broom in hand, remarked to the girls that it was one of the fundamental principles of good house-keeping to keep a bright hearthstone; that a slovenly-kept hearth had sent many a man to a well-kept saloon, and the wife, left weeping by the dirty hearth, never guessed the reason why.

"But, mother, there is not a saloon on the Pacific Coast. How could we go to one, even if the dirt were knee-high about our hearth?" inquired the future statesman, Thomas Ames.

Mrs. Murdstone, who like her son, had a logical mind, answered: "My dear boy, if the rumors we hear of the gold mines in California, are true, not one year will elapse until our primitive exemption from that evil will be but a thing of the past, and we shall not even remember that there was a time in the early history of Oregon when we were a strictly temperance people, because we had not a drop of whisky in the whole territory, unless a small quantity in some private medicine chest."

Thomas had been presented by his friend with a beautiful broadcloth cloak, reaching nearly to the ground, its chief attraction consisting of a deep circular cape, lined with satin. He used to toss this mantle over his shoulder, in a truly Cæsarian style, when he wished to enforce an argument upon Jean and his mother. Standing in the middle of that puncheon floor, manly as ever Cæsar did when on that summer's night in his tent he first put his mantle on, Thomas tossed back his mantle till the soft folds of cloth and satin glistened in the fire-light's glow, as he said: "I believe those stories are true, and more than ever has been told us, of the gold nuggets of California, and I'm not going to stay around here and plow a field in the day-time and sit droning over a book at night, dear mother, and let the other fellows walk off with bags of gold, if your hearthstone is the dearest and cleanest that ever a fire blazed upon. That's why I'm going to visit the Mission to-night, to see Mr. Marshall, who says he will help three of us boys to go on the return trip of the sailing vessel that goes out next week." And picking up a broom splinter he carelessly tossed it with his thumb into the fire, then walking to the door, he said, "I shall not be gone more than two hours to-night, but I hope, to make all the arrangements for my final departure," and he was on his pony and gone before his mother could say a word. She rather fell than sat into the nearest chair. "He is so young, not yet seventeen years old; so delicate; so handsome; can I, oh, Jean, can I part with him!" the poor mother moaned.

CHAPTER XV.

THE CALIFORNIA GOLD-DIGGER.

The Hudson Bay Company's traders had a post at Vancouver, situated on the banks of the Columbia River, at the point where the Willamette River's bright water meets the majestic Columbia and flows on peacefully to the sea. The small sailing vessels belonging to this company ventured across the Columbia bar and sailed up the broad waters, scaring the wild geese, duck, and deer, and making the savages scud over the water in their swift, darting canoes, to seek shelter in the dense forests that cover the banks and stretch away for hundreds of miles into the interior. Even these little vessels came only twice a year, bringing supplies to the company, which were meager enough in variety, but excellent in quality. These vessels, on their return to New York, were laden with furs that the traders had bought from the Indians. They were furs of the otter, mink, beaver and bear, elk, deer, and sometimes a buffalo robe. It was on one of these outgoing sail-vessels that Thomas Ames, with a company of about twenty others, went to seek his fortune in the gold mines.

Our pioneers found the winters of '48 and '49 very mild, warm and rainy. Nearly every day a slight mist fell, and nearly every day the sun shone out brightly, making the little birds twitter, the wild flowers bloom, and the grass spring up green and fresh, very much like spring in the East. The stately fir trees proudly wore their green boughs the year round; the only change they deigned to make was that each year, after the propitious rains had washed their dark evergreen boughs bright, they fringed the tips of each waving bough with a new growth two inches deep of a light pea-green color.

This is the dignity they maintain for a hundred years or more, as long as they live standing in those mighty forests, throwing off no leaf nor bark—on and on the steady growth. Thousands, if not millions, of acres of these giant trees standing so close, they are locked in each other's arms, beneath whose shade it is dark as night—the sun never penetrating—no bud, bush nor blossom can grow beneath them. The rich, loamy earth is soft, like a carpet to the tread, but bare as a floor of all other growth. Every valley of Oregon is dotted with these stately sentinel evergreen fir trees; every river has its banks lined with these trees. In the mountains are the hemlock and cedar, and along the water-courses the alder, ash, maple and beautiful oak quarreling for the mastery, but the fir tree stands its ground like a thing of power and exceeds them all; while the curly maple, as though angry at the wrongs done it, has curled and gnarled and knitted itself into so many beautiful lines while growing, that it is the handsomest wood in the world. Fine-grained, and, like some people, susceptible of high polish, it should take rank among the finest woods. Even so early as '48, the missionaries had a turning-lathe, and constructed furniture out of this beautiful curly maple, and Mr. Murdstone secured some before the prices leaped up, as everything did in '49 after the discovery of gold. Who can tell how these fir trees obtained their mastery, or for how many thousands of years they have held sway over valley, hill-top and mountain, lined the deepest canyon's side, and stood on the highest mountain range, or what element in the soil produces this masterful tree? Their roots spread into the soft earth just as far as their boughs spread into the air, and they penetrate the earth very deeply, the giant stems shooting up into the air to a height of from two to three hundred feet. They are wonderful trees, these monopolists of the great Northwest! If the prairies of Illinois and Missouri are awe-inspiring, what must be the feeling that takes possession of a soul contemplating the width, the length, the depth of these endless forests?

Jean Ames, though a child as she was, stood wrapped in a dream, thinking of the great plains, the vast forests, and the mighty sea, on whose bosom you may ride forever, and it is still the great, mysterious, wonderful sea. Jean was looking in the direction of the sea, that lay a hundred miles to the west, wondering if her brother Thomas would not return, bringing his bags of shining gold. She thought that he had only to go to the mines and pick up gold as one would pick up kernels of corn that were scattered on the ground, and some of the nuggets were as big as her thumb, she had been told. If this could be so, the deepest longing of her heart would be realized, and she would go to the Mission boarding-school. No girl should outrank her in learning. Jean had shed many bitter tears when her father's library was sold. How she longed to be in the society of scholars; and if Tom should come, he and she would go to school together. How promising and bright life was to her that day.

This bright cup of bliss, that Jean vainly hoped for, was not the one that was offered her that day, but instead, the bitterest dregs that a woman's lips could taste. While she still stood looking, a man appeared coming over the hill leading a horse. It was not her brother; it was too tall a figure. The man had a loose, shambling gait, and in every way was ungainly. He could not be her brother, who was a young man, straight as an arrow, nimble as a deer, and graceful in every movement as a young fawn. The man gave his hat a twitch every few moments as he walked along, turned to glance at his horse, and made a quick, eager survey of the country about him. All this attracted Jean's attention, and she called her mother, and they together stood watching him till he made his way straight to the house. He still held his horse, and walking up to the gate, asked Mrs. Murdstone for permission to stop a day or two at her house.

"My name is Cursica Miser, and I own the adjoining land claim," he said, pointing awkwardly in the direction of the neighboring hills.

"My name is Carsien Miser, and I own the adjoining land claim."

Mrs. Murdstone and Jean exchanged quick glances, thinking it might be possible that they would hear from Tom; they would at least hear much that would interest them in regard to the mines, and would gladly have given him a warm welcome, but he declined, saying he would hold his horse until Mr. Murdstone came, and so remained at the gate. Mr. Murdstone coming soon, a long conference was held between the two gentlemen at the gate.

It ended in the stranger's uncinching his saddle-girth, and unfastening heavy loads, that were firmly tied to the pummel of his saddle on either side. One, he gave to Mr. Murdstone, laying another on the ground, while he disengaged the third. Then they cautiously removed the saddle, which proved to be a perfect arsenal of Colts' revolvers and bowie knives, and brought them to the house, and the horse with its bridle was sent by Dan Murdstone to the stable.

Mr. Murdstone brought the stranger into the house with his loads. There was a heavy solid oak chest stowed away under the rafters in this cabin chamber. It had a strong lock. Mr. Murdstone conducted the stranger to this room, and deposited the heavy bags of gold nuggets in the chest. The two gentlemen had to climb to the loft by the rounds of a ladder—the same primitive construction for ascending and descending that a hod-carrier uses. Without any preliminary arrangements with Mrs. Murdstone, the strange gentleman was installed in the house as a boarder for an indefinite period of time.

On being introduced to Mrs. Murdstone, he confided to her that, on account of the excitement of the gold-digging, his health had been very much "shottered," and he required a quiet country place and simple food to regain his usual composure. Mrs. Murdstone and Jean were very eager to know something of the hardships the miners endured, and something of the process of gold-digging. Mr. Miser seemed reticent on the subject, so Mrs. Murdstone had very little comfort from his remarks, and as dinner was to be prepared the two men were left to converse alone. After dinner the stranger took his horse and rode to his land claim to look over his possessions. He had gone, the summer before, with a company of packers overland from Oregon to California. The first $5,000 that he had picked up had been stolen by a company of Mormons, and the next rich vein he struck he decided to get away with, and bring it to a safe and quiet corner in Oregon, where he had already some interests. This he had told Mr. Murdstone in their confidence at the fence. Jean and her mother, being left alone in the house, after sitting thoughtfully for a moment Mrs. Murdstone remarked:

"I wish we were not such near neighbors to the California gold mines. Think of this strong man, after being gone only a few months, coming back and saying his nerves were all 'shottered'; think of poor Tom sleeping on the ground and having nothing to eat but beans and a little bacon, and he is such a child, and can't stand hardships like a man!" And Jean cried:

"Oh, mother, why couldn't it have been Tom come home with all that gold?" and the tears sprung to her eyes.

Mrs. Murdstone then thought of the gold with a repulsive shock, and said:

"Jean, I'm afraid to stay in the house. Our home is just spoiled. That stranger to be here at every meal, and we afraid of being murdered for his gold, while the men are away plowing in the field. But it is just as he says, there are no banks to put money into in this country."

"Well," answered Jean, "I'm not afraid. There are no robbers here. Were not the people who came with us across the plains some of the best people in the world? And there were no people here but a few Catholic and Methodist missionaries before we came, and they are not going to turn robbers, are they?"

CHAPTER XVI.

THE LAND LAW.

Mrs. Murdstone and Jean were sitting in a large airy room that was used for a bedroom, as well as a private sitting-room for herself and daughters. The house was constructed of logs of the young fir trees, which were well adapted for building log houses, as they shoot up tall, straight and slender. It was termed a double log house, having two rooms. Nearly all the early settlers confined themselves to a one-roomed house. This was eighteen by twenty feet, with chambers above each, used for sleeping apartments. The house was made more attractive, as well as more comfortable, by a board veranda running the full length of the front of it. The back of the house also had a veranda, which was made very convenient by being clapboarded up one side, and used for a kitchen. The doors were made of clapboards, and windows it had none, and yet the daylight was never entirely excluded. The many cracks between the logs admitted the daylight, and often the sunlight. There were puncheon floors that were made from boards that were split instead of sawed; they were generally about a foot wide, ten feet long, and two inches thick, but, like some people's word, there was very little accuracy about them. The clapboards were made of trees that split nicely; they were usually four feet long, from eight to ten inches wide, and intended to be half an inch thick. These were laid on the roof, in the same manner as shingles, but as there were no nails in the country, they had to be fastened to the roof with long poles, which gave the house a somewhat rude and picturesque appearance. This abode was situated near the center of their section of land, which had a southern exposure on a gently sloping side-hill. Just back of the house was a beautiful grove of fir, pine and maple trees, with a sprinkling of alders; just enough to show that there was a spring of water flowing from the ground, which made quite a little brook, that ran along about a mile, and lost itself in the rich loam of the soft, black earth. Here the Murdstones made a garden, and on the banks of this little rivulet they planted an orchard of apples; and higher on the ground, where the hill was more sandy, they planted peach trees. But all this planting happened after the time of which we write, when Jean and her mother sat in the privacy of their own room, deploring the intrusion of a stranger into their family. Mrs. Murdstone, smiling at Jean's simple faith in the honor of the early settlers, said:

"Oh, well, the Bible teaches us to be good to strangers, as we may entertain angels unawares."

"Does it caution us against entertaining strangers, lest we entertain devils unawares?" queried Jean. Could they have known the truth about the stranger, they would have been more loth to entertain him than they were.

"Well, Jean, I must go and prepare the evening meal, as it is now half past four."

And Jean answered pettishly: "I wish our land claim was ten miles wide, so that the neighbors could not come and impose upon us by asking to be boarded." Now the homestead that Mr. Murdstone had selected from out the vast domain of Uncle Sam's territory seemed small, when compared to the miles and miles of unoccupied land that lay adjacent thereto. But it had been agreed upon by the early settlers that they would each claim a mile square of the public land, and that their first representative to Congress would be loaded up and shipped around the Horn with that one idea, that one message from his constituents to Congress asking to give them a title to their land. This was no small undertaking, when one considers that those old statesmen from Rhode Island, Delaware and New Hampshire, could not entertain the idea for a moment that a man could ask for a piece of land for a farm that was almost as large as their State. But Samuel R. Thurston found broader men who represented Texas and Missouri, and the broad prairies of the west, and succeeded in securing the passage of the bill that gave to each early settler his six hundred and forty acres of land. It was upon Samuel R. Thurston's shoulders that the mantle of congressional honors first fell, placed there by that spartan band of heroes, the pioneer men who laid the foundation of the proud State of Oregon. No statesman ever filled his honored post with greater zeal; no one's return was looked forward to with more eager anticipation, nor warmer welcome ever awaited a man returning to the people he had served. But he did not live to receive this welcome, as on his return he was smitten with the Panama fever which proved fatal. His remains were brought back, and every honor conferred that affection could give to the noblest man that ever served the state, or perhaps ever will.

One of the noblest features of the land law was that one-half of each grant was given to the women. No single man could hold more than three hundred and twenty acres of land, which placed all the marriageable women in the territory at par value immediately. Many an old bachelor brushed up his best suit of clothes, and hied him to see the fairest lady in the land. Like many other good laws, it could be turned to bad account. If a man was unmarried, he could hold only one-half of the six hundred and forty acres of land. This law extended over a term of years. Men, in order to hold the land claim they had staked out for themselves, would hunt for a wife pretty lively, or some other old bachelor could settle on one-half of his land claim. Girls of twelve and fourteen, and in some cases, only eleven years of age, were married in the years of '49 and '50, to men twice, and sometimes three times their own age. Now, to the great credit of the parents, and the men who contracted with these parents for these young girls for their wives, sometimes only the ceremony of marriage was enacted. By this arrangement, the girls secured the land, and then they were allowed to remain at home with their parents, sent to school, and grew to womanhood before the marriage rites were consummated.

Hazardous as this must have been to the future happiness of these fair young girls so entrapped, it was an infinitely better condition of affairs than the fate of those young girls who were taken by the marriage rites by these selfish men, claimed as wives, just as the land was claimed by them simply as a convenience. What man, building a home on such broad acres, did not need a slave to do his cooking, washing, general housekeeping, as also a wife, all in one and the same person? How convenient! What an excuse, when Congress, the government of the United States, the solons of the country, the picked men of the nation, selected for their wisdom, learning and far-reaching insight into the well-being of the people in whose interest they were called upon to legislate, had given them such a bribe! Three hundred and twenty acres of land with a wife, were not found every day. The land and wife were theirs to all intents and purposes, so they thought, for in those days men thought a woman only a toy or a slave for him. The idea had not permeated the brain of the average man yet that woman was an independent, sentient being, apart from him. She was his, to be, to do, to suffer, whatever he dictated. We shall see, notwithstanding the sanction of the accumulated' wisdom then in Congress assembled, what the results were, at least in some cases, of this wise land law.

Mr. Cursica Miser was one of those gentlemen who had a broad land-claim and no wife. He could not endure the idea of seeing his noble section of land split in two. It was not half large enough as it now lay. To cut it in two would spoil his future pastures, his grain-fields, his orchards and building site. He could not see another man taking half his possessions— not he. "Congress was full of old cranks that did not know a thing about a new country. They ought to know that a man without a wife made just as good a citizen as a man with a wife, and what idiots to pass a law that a man should marry, when there are no women in the country, or be robbed of half his possessions. But law is law, if there isn't an atom of sense in it." Thus debated Mr. Cursica Miser. "And now, Rainbow, we 'must scour the hills and hunt for heifers. No cattle to be driven to-day, old Rainbow," and he mounted his swayback steed, whose peculiar anatomical formation had earned him this soubriquet, and away they swept, over hill and down dale, until they came to the nearest cabin, where lived a very poor man who had three marriageable daughters, together with his wife and three small girls and a boy baby. The mystery was, how the family ever got across the plains. The secret was, a rich relation had helped them start, and the company had helped them on, and lo! the wheel of fortune had brought luck to their very door, and what glorious luck when Mr. Miser passed *by* their cabin door. Seeing the ponies tied near by, he said to himself, "This is not the time to call there. I will just go down this hill, across the creek, and see if old Shrum's girls are at home, or if they are besieged by land-claim hunters, too, as Olinger's daughters are. He is in luck, at least; those three girls will every one hold some fellow's land-claim for him. They are not bad-looking girls, either, are they, old Bow?" And he leaned forward and stroked his horse's mane. The horse shot forward, hearing a gallop behind him, and the rider was soon by Miser's side. The two men bowed and both reined their steeds at Mr. Shrum's gate. Mr. Chas. Gibson was the man that the fair Eufamie was awaiting on her father's broad porch. Thus it was that Mr. Cursica Miser found himself vanquished on every side. He twitched his hat to Miss Eufame, bowed to her mother, asked for a drink of water, twiched his hat again to the company, was on his horse and gone out of sight and out of mind sooner than it takes to tell it.

The next morning Mr. Cursica Miser and Mr. Murdstone held another long discussion at the gate. Mrs. Murdstone said to Jean, "What can those men be plotting about? No good, I'll warrant. I feel there's something wrong. I wonder if the steamer has brought news of Thomas. It's something they're arranging before they tell us. What can it be, Jean? I am overwhelmed with apprehension. I fancied last night, that Mr. Miser kept looking at you out from under his broad-brimmed hat. I don't like that peculiarity in the man of looking out from under his eyebrows."

"I don't like any of his looks," returned Jean. "But I don't know what he is to us that we need care for his 'tricks and his manners,' and I don't see why you need care, mother, if two men stood and talked at the gate till doomsday. Like St. Paul: 'I thank God I am not like other men,' and that I was not born a coward. 'Sufficient unto the day is the evil thereof,'" and she put her arm around her mother and kissed a tear away. "There, the conference is finished, and each man is going his own way. Dry your tears, dear mother."

CHAPTER XVII.

"THE MAN LET THE NUGGETS FALL SOFTLY BACK."

If the reader will go back to Mr. Shrum's porch, and listen to the lovers' talk, this is what they will hear them say. "I hope that man, Mr. Miser, doesn't visit here?"

"No, Charles, not often; Mr. Miser has just returned from the gold mines; did you meet him there?"

"Well, no, not exactly. I did not meet him, but he met my revolver. No man was ever truer named, and yet mothers are so anxious to have their daughters married to rich men, that some poor girl will get wofully taken in by that wretch yet. Why he was too mean to eat beans up on Feather River last fall, and the boys all got down on *me* because the cuss came from the same territory. Why every man on the bar despised Oregon because he was so mean, suspicious and stingy. He was glad enough to leave Feather River and go to Mormon Island. They would have hanged him if he hadn't left the very day he did, and I would have been glad to help pull the rope, and twice glad if I ever thought he would come between you and me, Eufamie. He would starve his wife and strangle his children because they had to eat."

"Charles Gibson, are you sure what you say is true?" asked Eufamie, looking grave for a moment, as with a shudder she thought of the time she had seriously contemplated becoming Mrs. Miser herself.

"Yes, I am sure. Mining life brings out a fellow's real character as nothing else ever can. You remember, Eufamie, that I wrote you a letter telling of the death of poor Martin Farnsworth. Everybody tried to keep that poor fellow alive. You see he had been out prospecting; he was lithe as a cat, with a hand fair as a woman's." Here Charles took Eufamie's little, plump hand, patted it, and stooping gracefully as a courtier, carried it to his lips, and so absorbed was he, thinking of the fate of poor Martin, that a tear fell on Eufamie's hand. It was that tear that won the hesitating girl to his side. Without seeming to notice the tear that silently fell, a tribute to the memory of Martin Farnsworth, the boy geologist, who kissed his widowed mother a last farewell in New York six short months before, Charles went on: "Martin knew the rocks, the names of everything about them; he knew the gold-bearing quartz, the placer mining, the gulch digging, and everything, for he had studied what other men had found out about mining in other countries, and had put into books; he located our diggings where we struck it rich. One morning, Mart said to me: 'Charles, I am going to find out how far up these gulches a fellow can find gold; I'm going to the head of this, and prospect every inch of ground.' I said: 'Mart, you've got a good pile now. If I were you I'd be getting out of these mountains back to my poor old mother.' But Mart said: 'Charley, that's my mother's address,' handing me a scrap of paper, 'you see that she has my pile, if anything should turn up,' and he looked down soberly at his feet for a minute. He was a handsome fellow, tall and shapely as you would see among a thousand men. The clouds were sailing along half way up the mountain side. Mart looked up and said: 'Charley, look for me above the clouds in two hours from now.' 'Yes,' said I, 'and if a grizzly prospects you, let's hear your gun talk, and I will be with you, Mart.' I could hear his merry whistle, Eufamie, and I can hear that whistle yet whenever I shut my eyes. Poor Mart walked straight to his death. He got lost and was out all night. There came a deep snow. He had found a grizzly, shot at it, only wounding it, and then followed a fierce contest with the wounded beast, and at last he succeeded in getting his revolver into the enraged

brute's mouth, and shooting twice into his throat killed
the terrific monster. We tracked the grizzly and found
Martin, torn, mangled. God! what a sight. He was
lying there by the bear, having drunk its warm blood,
and so kept alive. We brought him, laid as carefully
as we could in a blanket, down that awful mountain side.
It was a three miles' walk around the side of the
mountain, and I never let go my end of the blanket.
Poor fellow, it hurt him so if we stumbled over a
stick or stone, or jostled him in the least, or didn't
hold him on a level, which was a very difficult thing to
do on a steep mountain side. The bear lay there with
one half of the skin torn from its body. Mart said he
pulled the hide of the beast over him to keep from
freezing to death. 'His old carcass,' boys, he said, 'kept
warm until most morning. I was afraid the wolves
would come, boys, before you found me, or I should
have shot every ball from the revolver, only for the
horror of being eaten alive by these cannibal wolves.
It was dark when the bear came at me; do you see that
leg? He tore that first, then let his paws sink into
the flesh, and stripped it from the bone. I shot him
in the shoulder; then he let that paw sink into my back,
that made me sick for a minute. He reared back and
let his paws fall here.' And we could see the bone of
his arm from the shoulder to the elbow, all bare, Eufamie—it was sickening."

Eufamie had her apron to her eyes.

"There were twenty men gathered about him in a
minute, and twenty guns were fired as soon as we heard
him speak, and knew he wasn't dead. We had agreed
on the morning before we left camp, to fire twenty guns
if we found him alive, ten if dead. Our guns spoke of
Mart's being alive to a thousand anxious men who had
dropped pick-axe and shovel to scour hill-side and
mountain for the brave man who had been the most
successful prospector in camp. Mart had torn up his
shirt and tied up his leg very well, better than we
thought he could, with his wounded arm, but he had
only crowded the wound together on his back as well

as he could, and lay there on his face with the bearskin drawn tightly over him; the snow was covered with blood all round. When we took the poor fellow up there wasn't a dry eye among us. Mart said: 'Boys, I knew you would come. Don't ever let mother know this. It will soon be all over with me.' He lived three days. We buried him under the pine close by camp. The wolves couldn't get him there, and in the spring just when I left, we put him in a rough box, sent it down to 'Frisco, and shipped it home to his mother.

"The second day we brought him into camp, it was plain to everyone he couldn't live. He got restless, the fever grew high, he kept saying, 'Mother, mother!' and we knew he was getting delirious. Mart had helped to locate the diggings, you see, so we took up a collection. His pile amounted to $7,000, and we added three, making $10,000. I weighed it, poured it into a big gold-quartz pan, and, showing it to him, told him what we had done. The tears came into his eyes, he choked up, and tried to say 'mother.' He lay still a long time, then, with a great effort, tried to speak, and we gathered this, 'God save you boys, from death in the mountains——hard to die among one's friends—— but this is harder. You have blunted my agony by your generosity to my mother.' He soon fell into a stupor and never spoke again." Here Charles broke down utterly, and let the tears stand on his eyelids, but seeing Eufamie couldn't speak for fear her voice would betray the emotion the story had awakened, roused himself, and pursued: "When we were taking up the collection for Martin's mother, I went to Miser myself. I was sure he wouldn't give anything, and he didn't. He whined out an excuse that he didn't pan out anything that day. In the evening, just at sundown, when the remains of poor Martin were already in the rough box where we had laid him, and the men had come to take a last look at their dead comrade, Jim Gregory said, 'Pals, we've no flowers to place about him, but let us cover his coffin with evergreen boughs, to show that our memory for the noble hero who has lost his life in our common cause—hunting for gold—will ever be green, and to show that his efforts were not in vain, place the pan of gold on the coffin, letting every man in camp take heart that though death meet him, his labors will not be lost to the friends he loves!' We did as Gregory had suggested, covered the coffin with evergreen boughs, and set the pan of gold in the center to remain all night. We put six picked men at the foot of the coffin near the camp-fire, as watchers. We, that had been his most intimate friends, rolled ourselves in our blankets and lay down to rest for the night. We were worn out with watching. That morning at about four o'clock I saw a man crawl along on all fours stealthily like a cat, and, reaching out his long fingers, almost touch the pan that held the nuggets. I held my breath, everything was still as death, the fire had burned to embers. There was a faint star-light, I could hear the men breathing heavily, I thought — God forgive me — that it was Jim Gregory. But at that moment one of the watchers stretched his legs, yawned, wrapped his blankets about him, and soon snored again. At the moment he did so, the man let the nuggets fall softly back, flattened himself on the ground, and turned his face full to mine. I saw him plain as I see you this minute, Eufamie. I was in the corner of the cabin where it was dark, and it was evident that he did not see me. It was Miser. I yawned to make believe I had just waked up, turned over and called to Jake Foley, who sat on a stool in the corner near me, to stir the fire. Then Jake and I talked now and again till morning."

Eufamie turned her tear-stained eyes full upon Charles Gibson, saying, "Why didn't you call the camp and have him hanged?"

"Why, Eufamie, what could I do? There we were, all rolled in our blankets on the ground. A dozen men might have reached out their hands the same as he did. I knew no one saw him but me. The act could not be reproduced if I had called the camp, and there was no proof. If I had not happened here just as I did, in half an hour he would have asked you to be his wife, the villain!"

"He would never have asked me to be his wife, for I should not have given him the opportunity," was the spirited reply of Eufamie.

No words could have passed the proud girl's lips that could have given her lover more delight, and yet he seemed all unconscious, and went on to say: "We sent the gold to his mother, but what recompense could that be in her old age, compared with the companionship and care of such a son. Miser was the only man in camp who did not put an ounce of gold in the pan to make up the sum," and Charles Gibson's wrath increased like an avalanche as he continued: "That villainous Miser is rightly named; he will go and ask some woman to marry him, just to save his land claim. It may be a young girl; or, if he can't get a white woman he will marry a squaw, and I pity the squaw, for there is not one on the Pacific coast but is infinitely his superior. Such a base villain as that ask a woman to marry him, to secure his land claim! There is no baseness on earth that he would not stoop to for gain."

"I am afraid you are not inclined to be charitable towards Mr. Miser," smilingly returned Eufamie, looking intently at an old hen and chickens that were scratching gravel a few feet away.

"Charity! I hope not. If I had, I should hate myself as I hate him now. The sight of the man has spoiled my afternoon with you. I came here intending to tell you the deepest desire of my heart, but now I think I shall wait three years, until this land law is extinct. I would not be such a craven for worlds as to ask a woman to marry me simply to secure a piece of government land."

Eufamie, without stopping to think what the import of her words might be, said, "No one would ever accuse you of such a thing."

Charles Gibson passionately took her hand in his and asked, "My dear girl, would you not in three days' time be looking questioningly into my eyes to know whether I had asked you to be my wife for love or land?"

And Eufamie, answering, said, "Never, Charles, could I impute a dishonorable motive to you."

"My dear girl, if that be really true, will you be my wife?"

"Gladly, Charles," she answered, "if there were not a foot of land in the whole world."

"We'll be happy, Eufamie, and never think of old Miser again while we live. Such words, Eufamie, from the lips of a woman that a man loves ought to make him feel prouder than a king, when amidst deceit, falsehood and the basest fraud, a man may so conduct himself that no one can impute a wrong motive to his acts. Surely, Eufamie, you are my better self that holds the mirror of my inmost soul, reflecting the noblest instincts of my being. Sweet girl, will the rest of your family and our neighbors read my heart and acts as royally as you do? You are all the world to me, and they shall read my acts by your interpretation; and since you will it so, government lands shall not hasten or hinder our marriage vows, my love." And Charles Gibson clasped the fair form of Eufamie to his manly heart, to be sheltered there forever.

And thus we leave the honest, happy pair, to see what discoveries we can make by observing the mysterious maneuvers of Mr. Cursica Miser, some days having elapsed since we saw him so abruptly leave the fair Eufamie to the tender care of Mr. Charles Gibson. Long conferences had been held at the gate by Miser and Murdstone. Mrs. Murdstone's anxiety was daily increasing. Not a syllable had been spoken to her by her husband of what was the subject of these long talks. Oh, how she appreciated her far-away friend, Doctor Knight. What would she not give for an hour's advice from him! She was sure there was some evil hatching, and yet she was ashamed to suspect her husband. If there was not some mischief brewing, then why so much mystery? Jean was quick to lay bare her step-father's acts with scathing criticism. This made Mrs. Murdstone bear more patiently the torture she was undergoing than she otherwise would. If Jean understood that these long talks between Miser and Murdstone caused her mother anxiety, she would fearlessly speak to them, which would put the gentlemen on their guard, and Mrs. Murdstone would thereby lose any possibility of gaining a clue to their mysterious plotting, and thus be deprived of the opportunity of defending herself. And so Mrs. Murdstone passed her days in watching and her nights in sleepless vigil.

After this plotting had been going on for a week or two, one morning Mrs. Murdstone arose with eyes so swollen and red with weeping that she could not appear at the breakfast table. Jean had to take her mother's place. She was wrathful. She had begun to surmise that those two men who sat opposite her were the cause of her mother's grief, and she poured out vengeance along with the coffee, which was not wholly unobserved by the two gentlemen. She saw some telegraphic dispatching to each other from the eyes of the gentlemen. When her duty was over she excused herself without tasting a morsel, and went in search of her mother. She found her in her bed-room and on her knees, her bible open beside her, pouring out her soul in supplication to God to spare her from this great trial, to spare Jean to her for years to come. "As I am merciful and tender to the little orphan girls intrusted to my care, be Thou tender, oh, Father in heaven, to my little one. She is dearer to me than my own life. Spare her; oh, Father, spare me!" There she broke into such loud sobbing her whole frame trembled, and she could no longer speak. Jean, who had crept softly in, heard these last few words of pleading. She could not endure this, and knelt beside her mother, saying, "I am with you, mother; what is the matter? Nothing shall hurt me. See, I am here, and will be always." Then the sobbing broke out again like a storm that would not be stayed. Her tears fell on Jean's hair and neck, and trickled down her back.

This made Jean wrathful again, and she sprang to her feet like a young lioness, exclaiming, "Mother, mother, get up and stop crying! This will never do! You will be sick and die, and I shall be the one that is left alone. This would kill anybody. I would not cry like that for all the men that ever lived."

"Nor I, my child, but for you, and your poor dead father, how he would have protected you; your brothers, so far away, and all my kith and kin, all our dear friends. In one deluge of tears I weep for all these woes; having suffered, I dread the tortures that are to come, and so I weep. Poor, poor child, you are so young."

"I was younger yesterday, and you did not weep. There must be some other cause. Has my noble stepfather at last consented that I shall attend the Mission boarding-school?"

"No, child, it is not that; how gladly would I have you attend that school."

"Why don't you be strong, mother, as I am; don't ask God to make you strong, but be strong, say; 'Jean goes to school,' and that would end all the trouble. When I am a woman, mother, I'll not deluge my grief with tears, and if anybody makes me cry what do you think they'll be doing?"

Here a faint smile lighted Mrs. Murdstone's face, as she said: "Oh, Jean; I hope God will not send such trials to you, but 'whom God loves he also chasteneth.' Let us kiss the rod."

"Oh, no, mother; I'm not the 'kissing-rod' kind."

Then Jean persuaded her mother to bathe her face in cold water, and gave her some coffee and tucked her up in bed, saying half to herself, "When you awake we'll see what can be done to rid the house of its pest."

Next morning the usual conference was not held at the gate, but at the farthest end of the field, a half a mile away. The old horse stood in the furrow for two long hours, while the two gentlemen sat on the top rail of the fence and talked.

Mr. Cursica Miser had decided to go on a fishing

and hunting excursion to the mountains for a couple of months. He had told Mr. Murdstone to cautiously ascertain from his wife what the chances would be for him to secure the hand of Jean in marriage.

"The man let the nuggets fall softly back."

CHAPTER XVIII.

THE MAIDEN'S SACRED BOWER.

Jean's manner at the breakfast table, and Mrs. Murdstone's non-appearance on the preceding morning, caused Mr. Miser to decide in his own mind that he would abandon the idea of asking that proud little minx to share his lordly wealth. He said to himself, "I would rather marry a squaw; I could beat her every day, and there would be no resistance." But he did not say so to Mr. Murdstone. He simply told him to explain to his wife that he had gone away, and when he did return he would most likely be a married man. Jean's mother had to keep her bed for several days, and most of the work for the large family devolved upon Jean. Her moments for reading, recreation or rest were few, but she did try each day to snatch a half hour to kneel in prayer in her leafy bower that she had made for herself, in a grove of trees that sheltered the spring, with its bubbling fountain of pure, sparkling water. Just before you came to the spring, the path that led to the house had been cut through the tangled wild vine-maple that grows about three inches in diameter. It runs on the ground, twists and turns, and locks itself back and forth, and finally ends in a tangled mass of leaf and bough, ten or fifteen feet high. No wild beast can make a path through a grove of vine-maple. But Jean, by bending some of the less refractory boughs, had penetrated a rod or two from the path into this deep seclusion, where she had constructed a rude altar and covered it with long silky mosses that grow on the fir-trees of that region. No sunlight could enter, and the little daylight that came flickering in through the leaves made the place as solemn as a sanctuary in some dim old cathedral.

The girl had just room to kneel. If she moved, after getting into the quiet nook, the leaves would brush her hair and almost startle her as though they were living things that knew she came to worship there. They would taunt her with her ignorance and unworthiness. She, a little orphan child, dare to bend in the presence of Almighty God, the Ruler of the universe, the mighty Potentate of all power; who made the earth, set the stars in the heavens, lighted all with sun and moon, and these mighty orbs were the same that lighted all the land in the East, as well as in the far West. Jean could not utter a word aloud, but was every day surprised to find how her thoughts would flow in her silent prayer to God. Every day she asked for wisdom, even as Solomon had asked to be endowed with wisdom above his fellows.

"Oh, God, grant me wisdom above the women of my day; teach me what is right, and when I know the right, help me to be strong to do right always."

Just as Jean had finished these words, she heard footsteps, and in a moment Mr. Miser was saying to Mr. Murdstone, "I'll loan you all the money you want to improve your place for the next two years, and charge you no interest, but we must, in some way, keep Mrs. Murdstone in ignorance of this land law, or she will suspect our motives." Mr. Murdstone answered, "You can rely on me. I will do all in my power to make my wife look favorably upon your suit. But there! Don't say another word. I see the water-bucket at the spring, and Jean is somewhere near." The two men turned and walked back to the house, and Jean heard no more. She stepped cautiously out of the bower, then stooped and dipped her bucket into the water that was nearly as deep as a well, and mirrored back her features as clearly as any looking-glass. She often lingered over the curb to catch the outlines of her face that were as fine as chiseled marble.

But this time she hastened with her bucket, brimful of the sparkling water, to her mother, and told her what she had heard. The words meant nothing to Jean, but to her mother they were clear as crystal, and gave her an insight into the premeditated arrangements of the two men, as perhaps no other words could have done.

The next day Mr. Miser started off on his fishing and hunting excursion. The restful quiet that came to that house proved a blessing indeed to Mrs. Murdstone, who, having the tension taken off her nerves, was soon restored to her usual health. The Murdstones were happy for the next two months, laying plans for improving their large tract of land, dividing it into fields for wheat, oats, gardens, orchards, pastures for the calves, pastures for the milk-cows, oxen and work-horses. The potato-patch and bean-field all had to be considered, and the right place to be selected for each. The pasture must have running water, and, as there was a creek running through the entire length of the east and south sides, this question settled itself. But, not understanding the exact quality of land, or the conditions of climate that the grain-fields and orchards required, it took many a talk and many a walk before the best location could be decided upon. But there was still the more important question crowding itself upon that little community—that of building a school-house that would answer for a church as well. As the large front-room at the Murdstone's was always neat, commodious and cheerful, the neighbors had already met there several times to hold a kind of church service. Mr. Murdstone read the scriptures in a clear, strong voice, and Mrs. Murdstone was gifted in prayer, as also that rarest of womanly charms, a fine contralto voice, that could sing "Nearer, My God to Thee," or "Jesus Lover of My Soul," in tones that would melt a heart of stone, and draw sinners to worship *her*, if they did not their Father in heaven. So here they gathered to discuss the question of where they would build, how and when. Mr. Waldovere was the richest, and far the most learned man in the hills. He had been there the greatest length of time, but alas! he was a strong character, and would allow no man to dictate terms to him, certainly no preacher. He knew just as much about heaven and hell as they did, and he could consign his neighbors to one or the other place with equal facility. He said hell was invented by priests and kings to enslave their fellow-men. Waldovere and Murdstone would lock horns, and talk bible and history until the dinner was announced, when all differences were drowned in a fragrant cup of coffee, biscuit that would melt in your mouth, with butter that had the cream taste all left in; baked potatoes that were as mealy and light as flour; often, delicious wild venison; sometimes grouse, cooked with cream gravy; now and again, mountain trout, with their silver sides lightly browned; and to-day their dinner was finished with wild blackberry pie. If you have never eaten the wild blackberry of Oregon, dear reader, you must know that it is the best fruit that has ever been invented in nature's great chemical laboratory for making pies. Mr. Waldovere remarked to Mr. Murdstone, who sat next to him: "Your wife is a good cook, and there's not a d—— bit of step-mother about her. I don't believe she nor the children can tell which is which," and the happy children looked up with their mouths full, wondering what he meant. But the curly-headed baby Murdstone stuck itself under the tenderly caressing arm of Mrs. Murdstone, pouting out her lips defiantly, saying:

"You is my mamma," and the mother snuggling her up closer, says:

"Yes, Tot, you are my very own." Here they all laughed heartily, Waldovere saying: "No artist ever had so good a subject for a telling picture."

Before the gentlemen arose from the table, Mrs. Murdstone said she would like to be put on the building committee, and as men couldn't work without eating, she would do the cooking for them if Mr. Waldovere would promise to buy the lumber for the schoolhouse, which would be used for church services on Sundays:

"Father has about decided to give a five-acre lot where the broad-spreading oak trees make the place like a garden, and a part of the ground could be laid out for a cemetery."

Mr. Murdstone said, to himself: "It seems like sacrilege to use the same building for church and school."

And Mr. Waldovere, with a merry twinkle in his eye, remarked: "There are two of us against one, and if your scruples are so nice, you need not preach in the school-house; then it will not be desecrated," and with a hearty laugh, he won his point.

They walked to the building site, and decided between themselves where the lumber should be unloaded. Within less than six weeks a very substantial, commodious building was completed. The enterprise of the California gold mines had spread to the Territory of Oregon, and made it possible to put up a building made of lumber, with doors and windows, as early as the fall of '49.

It was the middle of October, and no teacher had yet been found. An Oregon mist was settling over the land,—something like a London fog,—but the people were paying no more attention to it than the Londoners do to their fogs; indeed, every avocation was being pushed with greater vigor, for these rains, or fine mists, were only a precursor of the long winter season that would soon set in "in dead earnest," as those pioneers used to say.

This bustle and increased activity made things seem very prosperous, and gave a cheerful, instead of a depressing influence, as one, far away, reading an account of those Oregon mists, might imagine.

Mrs. Murdstone was deep in the mysteries of the finishing touches of the rinsing, and wringing, rubbing and starching of the Monday's wash. No French laundry ever did better work, and this laundry work was done every week in the family, rain or shine. Mrs. Murdstone told her sons that, as manners made the difference between a gentleman and clown, so starch marks the well-bred from the common herd. But here we have no common herd, but starch, just the same, is very refining, and since it is so cheap, and life would be so drear without it, we will just use it freely, Jean." Another one of her practical home sayings was: "While we are about it, we will cook dinner enough for anyone who may happen in," and it seemed that the people sixty miles away would scent her dinners, for how they did "happen" along just before or just after dinner! To-day, the spare-rib and backbone of a fat pig had been served for dinner, the great heaping platter full had been set away, while a pile of nicely browned loaves from the Saturday's baking lay on the same shelf; near it, stood a roll of creamy butter. The dishes were piled in a big pan on the table, waiting to be washed, when a young man flung a long shadow on the floor, for the sun had shone out brightly that afternoon. Mrs. Murdstone wiped her hands from the white foam, stepped in to meet the shadow, bowed gracefully, and asked the young man to be seated. He was an intelligent looking young fellow of about twenty, with the tenderest down on his chin and upper lip, the mildest blue eyes, his teeth protruding when he smiled. He did not sit, but gave his hand to the matronly woman before him. Her warm grasp given him made them friends. In a clear, manly voice, he said: "I am too hungry to sit, Mrs. Murdstone. I have heard your name so often since I came into the neighborhood, that you seem like an acquaintance."

"I shall be glad to know you, I am sure, and since you are so hungry, you will not be dainty. The best man to feed is the man with an appetite, and as you cannot sit, just stand in front of my commissary stores and help yourself without ceremony, for my time is in great demand for the next hour, after which I shall be at leisure and happy to entertain you." And she opened wide her cupboard doors, stepped out on the open porch where her suds were awaiting her, and soon had the whole back yard, clear to the spring, lined with snowy linen.

The young man had done justice to the eatables he found in such generous quantity. He said he drank out of the five-quart milk-pan, cream and all. Poor fellow, young as he was, he had graduated from a law school in Iowa, and came out here to make a start in the world. Had crossed the plains with mule teams, arriving in the valley the last of August. He had intended to push right on to the gold diggings, but had plunged into the deep snow in the Rogue River mountain ranges, lying between Oregon and California; had subsisted on mule-meat for six days; had retraced his steps, and we find him in Mrs. Murdstone's larder, surrounding himself with plenty. His gold fever, he thought, had somewhat subsided, and he would be glad to teach the children in the new school-house for his board during the winter. But the old pioneers gave him a fair salary the first winter, and increased it and the number of children every year for five years. Then he married one of the noblest girls in the hills, not especially noted for her great beauty, but for her goodness. He won prominence as a lawyer in the State, and was sent as a representative to Congress for two consecutive terms, and was the father of a large and prosperous family of sons, his own fac-similes, with the same prominent teeth and generous smile.

CHAPTER XIX.

MARRYING FOR LAND.

With the virgin earth about them, with brave hearts and strong hands to carve out their fortunes in a new world, was it possible for these families to be other than hopeful and happy? And yet the worm will eat into the heart of the fairest rosebud, the brightest hopes vanish.

Mr. Miser returned, made an offer to Mrs. Murdstone for her daughter's hand in marriage, pressed his suit so fair and earnestly that Mrs. Murdstone wondered how she could have had a suspicion that he was not the soul of honor. She told Mr. Miser that if he could gain her daughter's consent, and wait two years for Jean, she would give him her consent. Mr. Miser was as timid and modest an accepted lover as a mother could desire, and at that interview, coincided with every wish the anxious mother could express; he showed wisdom in requiring Mrs. Murdstone to allow him sufficient time to make some impression on Jean's good-will, before she became aware of his intention of making her his wife, and with the utmost skill removed every trace of doubt from the mind of Mrs. Murdstone of his base motive of marrying Jean for the sake of securing his land, by assuring Mrs. Murdstone that he had been possessed of a deep and undying passion for her lovely daughter since the first day he saw her — she was so unlike any other girl. He had gone to the mountains to try to master this all-absorbing passion, but it had mastered him. He came again, and in his manly, frank way had determined to seek Mrs. Murdstone, and gain her consent to win the fair girl if possible. Oh, yes, he could wait five years, or ten, if at the end he was sure to win his prize. Mrs. Murdstone admired the ardent style of the man's pleading, but could not reconcile her conscience to acquiescing in Jean's marriage at this tender age; she soothed her troubled fears, nevertheless, by thinking "two years is some time. Jean will be sixteen, and she may refuse the man. Why should I feel so badly. After all, something may occur to interfere." And thus she allowed herself to be deluded, and so drifted down the smooth stream of time.

Now that the adroit Mr. Miser had removed all resistance, with his strong will, coupled with Mr. Murdstone's, they had swept away every objection, and instead of waiting two years, in less than two months, Jean Ames was Mrs. Miser.

Now, any girl of fourteen years, who was told to take her books, tie on her bonnet and go to school, would be most likely to do as she was bid; and so, when they bade Jean to be measured for her wedding gown, she said, "A new dress in this country is indeed a rare and lovely thing, but as for marrying that fellow, I don't think I ever will. I want to go to school. I don't want to be married so young. Other girls do not, and I shan't!" she protested poutingly.

Cursica Miser bought a little chestnut pony, and called it Jean's pony. He asked her to ride out with him. Jean took a brisk canter, and skimmed over the ground with as much ease as a bird sails through the air, and was home with her mother in half an hour. Mr. Miser beamed graciously upon her as he lifted her from the saddle, but not a word of love or marriage passed his lips. If there had, Jean would never have gone to ride again. Mr. Murdstone eagerly pointed out the advantages of such a marriage. She was the most fortunate girl in the whole country to be sought by a man of such wealth. "He is some years your senior, to be sure, but the wife grows older so much faster than the husband, that in point of fact your ages will be equal ten years hence." This cunning reasoning almost prevented the prospective marriage, for Jean argued,

"Why should I enter upon an arrangement of affairs whereby I shall grow old so fast?" and saying pettishly, "I shall not do it!" walked out of the room with a step light and free as the bounding deer on the mountain side, but with eye alert and head erect, very much as the deer that has heard the hunter's tramp or the hounds' yelp. What to do she did not know. Since her earliest recollection, every member of her family, when perplexed, sought refuge in prayer. Jean spent hours in her leafy bower, on her knees, asking God to direct her, and above all to give her wisdom to do right. "I am such a helpless child," she pleaded; "no father, no brother near, and my poor mother seems dazed and bewildered. Oh, God, spare me this fate! I want to go to school. I want an education like other girls. My soul is in rebellion. Oh, God, give me peace, and spare me this step in the dark! I know not what I fear. I know not why I so abhor this whole hateful affair from beginning to end."

If Jean had opened her heart to her mother, as she did silently to God in her prayer, it would have aroused her to action, and the poor child would have been saved. Jean thought she could not add trouble to her mother's already overflowing cup of bitterness, and silently, and somewhat heedlessly, glided on until the evil day set for the marriage arrived.

What could a child of fourteen know of the horrors of an unhappy mariage? The few guests, as they arrived, kissed her a merry good morning, saying she was a lucky girl, but her mother's pale face bore traces of tears, and the dear old minister, gray-haired, tender-hearted and good, wiped a tear from his eyes as he warmly pressed her hand. This alarmed Jean. She knew he loved her. She knew he was good and had more knowledge of what she was doing than she had. She was apprehensive, and asked Mrs. Morton, one of the elderly ladies, to walk with her to pick some flowers. They passed down the spring path that led to Jean's bower. Jean told her of the secluded spot, and said she had an intense longing to hide there until the day was passed. The woman looked surprised and grieved, but said: "My poor child, does your mother know how you feel?" Jean, pressing the grass with her dainty slipper, said: "No one knows but God."

"My child, your friends are older than you. We all have to trust our friends and family for our happiness. If I were you I would go on with the affair now as everything is in readiness. Every woman feels something as you do, at the last moment."

Jean's eyes dilated with rage, as she grew indignant at her hemmed-in condition.

"If I were a woman I would know my own mind and act it," and two great tears slid out from under her silken lashes, and trickled down her velvet cheek, in sympathy as much for all womankind who go trembling to their marriage vows, as in pity for herself. "Why should there be a chance for my being unhappy in married life, if all they have told me be true?" she queried. "Now, there is the minister, and my mother, the only people here who care for me at all, and they are both crying. I have a mind to run for my freedom, as the negroes do down south."

"My child," said Mrs. Morton, "you must trust your friends as older girls do; your mother, the minister, and all the people assembled at the house, have talked the matter over and over again. It is their opinion, evidently, that you are doing the best possible thing for yourself."

"Why is my mother so reluctant in giving her consent? Mr. Murdstone and Mr. Miser are the only ones eager for the union. If I should speak the truth to you I should say that neither of them ever intend to fulfill the contract they have made with my mother to gain her consent to this marriage. It is this, that I shall remain with her until I am seventeen; that she shall have a hired girl to do the work in my place, and Mr. Miser will pay the girl's wages; but when we do go to housekeeping, I shall always be provided with hired help, and that I shall not be subject to child-bearing until I'm twenty-five years of age. That, as Mr. Miser is abundantly able, he will always provide me with every comfort of life, and every wish, even for luxuries, shall be gratified. That sounds fine on paper, does it not? Let me tell you, when Mr. Miser first asked my mother to consent to our engagement he promised her faithfully that he would not ask that we be married before two years, because I am so young; and here he comes with an excuse that the government has made a land law that he did not know anything about at the time he asked for my hand; that every man shall be married or lose his half-section. Now, I want to remain a girl until I am a woman, and then marry a man, and not land. I have told them all this."

"But my dear, what a scandal you would create! Come, they are calling us now." Jean turned and walked slowly back to find the guests awaiting her.

CHAPTER XX.

THE MARRIAGE OF THE GIRL-CHILD.

Mr. Miser was an odd-looking man in his every day suit. But if anyone could have seen him in his wedding gear without smiling, they could do better than Jean did. There could be nothing wrong in the bride's smiling on the bridegroom, so the company thought, and the groom himself was pleased to see Jean looking so charmingly sweet.

Now, Jean herself was dressed like a matron of thirty, but this only enhanced her girlish appearance. It was the first time she had ever worn a long dress, which made her look taller and more womanly. But she could not walk with that ease and grace that she did in her short dresses. It was a brown alpaca, and the only piece of dress-goods to be found in the only dry-goods store in town.

There was absolutely no cloth in the store to make a suit for Mr. Cursica Miser, but after much perplexity, one of his bachelor friends sold him a piece of fine broadcloth that he had brought with him from the states. There was just enough in the piece to make himself a pair of pants. He was a very small man, and Mr. Miser much taller. But the tailor, hearing of the trials of the would-be bridegroom, promised to try to piece the cloth at both ends, and so, by dint of stretching, piecing, and Mr. Miser's "scrootching" a little, he thought it might be made to do duty as a pair of pants for a wedding suit. As Jean entered, Mr. Miser was standing in the middle of the floor talking to the minister, his lower limbs encased in the shiny broad-cloth. He was "scrootching" a little, as the man of art in constructing clothes had directed him to do. But, alas! for all the contracting he could do, the pants were determined to creep up above his shoe tops, and drop a little below his vest at the waist, so the white shirt looked like a sash peeping out between his upper and lower garments. If the coat had been big enough, Mr. Miser could have concealed this defect by buttoning one or two buttons at the waist.

Alas! for obstacles over which helpless man cannot triumphantly climb. The coat and vest in which Mr. Miser had decided to appear on his wedding day, had lain in his trunk since he was a young man of nineteen. He was now a man, with heavy beard, a sharp sprinkling of gray creeping into his side-whiskers. A man's form changes somewhat in all those years, though he may not have grown much stouter, and the coat that might have looked trim at nineteen, now utterly refused to make anything else of the man than a caricature. His shoulders being thicker, required more cloth to cover them, and this brought the seams of the waist high up under the shoulders, which made the coat-tail slightly elevated at the back. The front skirts tilted back to the side pockets of the pants, and left the expose of the quarrel between his pants and vest very prominent indeed, and as there was not a mirror large enough at that time in all Oregon, in which to see himself at full length, it was not at all probable that Mr. Miser could know what a grotesque figure he presented. Being a vain man, he would not have appeared before that company in that outfit for all the land in Oregon had he known just how he looked. He was, however, conscious of some defects in his attire, but when Jean appeared, and smilingly endured the sacrifice made for her by this ignorant and misguided people, he was seemingly complacent. How was it possible for a bible-reading, God-fearing, christian, civilized people to induce a child to enter the mystic horrors of marriage rites, that were so atrocious? It was possible at the time of which we write. If an unprotected family, on the extreme

But if anyone could have seen him in his wedding gear, without smiling, they could do better than Jean did.

frontier, **were shot and** tomahawked, **little children's brains dashed out against the stones, as, alas!** sometimes happened **in** those days, every**body could pale with horror at the** savage deed, **but they could see this innocent,** unsuspecting child **bound by the most galling chains of a** sacred **contract to a life instinct with** torture, **every** day **equal to** any ever **perpetrated by** the **savages; not a** death, with its quick still peace, **but life,** quivering with new horror and increasing **torture** each day. This is not the savage **blow** of revenge, but our highest, grandest, noblest Christian civilization, dealing with the key-note to the bulwark **of all** there is in life, the holy of all holies, the **family tie. The pure** girl of **fourteen, bound to the sensualist of forty-five,** in that **closest earthly tie, a marriage. Honest, cultured, thinking human beings could make laws to enable designing men to entrap a child into such a snare. Laws that intelligent people are** asked **to obey should be the culmination of perfection when worked** out in **the** great sum **of life, instead of developing all the** damning evil that fiends in hell would **pale** to enforce. **We are convinced, and think you will be,** who follow us, **that there were few girls ever born who** could stem the current of adverse **fate, beat back the scum** of crime, stay the fiery ordeal, **as did our brave and dauntless Jean,** and, **like the Hebrew children, come out without the smell** of fire **upon her** garments. **Let humanity forever** blush **that** could formulate **circumstances that would** make **life,** like the **one our pen tries, but will forever fail** to portray. **If a murder is committed before our** eyes and **we only smile, we give aid and sanction** to the **murderer, we abet the** crime. **There are** thousands **of crimes perpetrated** every day **upon our** fellows **that are worse than** taking their **lives, and yet, we are so stupid of the results** of **the many ultimate ramifications of these crimes, that we lend no voice nor force** against **them. How long, oh, Lord, will poor humanity** endure **its wrongs, and not even cry out for** redress?—**see its fellows fall daily, mowed down** like the tender grass, and still remain dumb as the beasts of the field?—not knowing every wrong they see committed, and lend no hand to relieve, raise no voice of protest, makes them aiders and accessories to the crimes; not even comprehending that the passive criminal is almost equal to the active one? Our pen should be sharp to prick the consciences of our fellows, so that other generations may have better conditions for the coming race than those that former days made for our heroine. It is time we had heroes and heroines in the strife, and not the patient dull-eyed cattle of the past that stolidly endured.

When Mrs. Murdstone found that she had made so irretrievable a mistake in assenting to this ill-assorted union—and every day made it more apparent—she was utterly prostrated with grief, and lay upon her bed for months, racked with the terrible pain of remorse. It came at the most critical period of a woman's life, when she hesitates, starts, fears and has no strength of resistance, as she had only a few years before. She often found herself sitting up in bed crying and wringing her hands in pitiable agony, trying in her sleep to bring Jean back to her again. It was the climacteric period with her. If she, or anybody about her, had understood her physical condition, all this frightful sickness and lamentable anguish could have been avoided. She would have said, "I require my daughter's companionship and she mine, until she is a woman grown. She shall marry no one until she is a fully matured woman, when she herself shall select her choice. I shall have nothing, absolutely nothing, to do with it." Murdstone and Miser would have looked elsewhere for a victim. If our laws were not weak, and not constructed by wholly incapable men, whose sensual lives have long since denuded their brains of the acumen that they otherwise would have possessed, our laws, would, of a surety, have strength enough in them to protect our girl-children from the sensual rapacity of men. The laws made for us by our wise brothers, that thrust marriage upon our child-girls, have worked a greater evil to the race than all the other crimes the world has ever committed. Our law-makers and physicians are the greatest criminals in making and sanctioning these laws. Then come the long-robed priests; but they are so well versed in the needs of the soul, and so little conversant with the requirements of the body, that they are to be excused somewhat. Our writers, brainless, superficial thinkers—the parents and stupid teachers of the race—such idiots! But the march of time will sweep them all out of our way like the flood-tide of a mighty river that carries forth the debris and dashes it to one side, here and there along its banks, covered with mud and scum and old dead leaves, rubbish of the past. Why do we punish evil-doers? Because they are doing harm to persons or property, which it is our business to protect. But we are always doing our punishing and protecting at the wrong end of society. We go among the lower classes, when we should go to the highest, where the power to do evil is the strongest.

What is the burning of an old barn, compared with spoiling the chances of a woman's life, and making it possible for her to produce a dozen or fifteen children, immature, half made up, imbecile, deformed, diseased, in every way robbed of what they have a right to—of health and strength and vigorous life? We all know that a child subject to the perils of maternity is not only destroying her own life, but making it utterly impossible for her to do else than produce feeble issue. If it is a crime to rob a child of half its existence, and make the half you do impart to it a weak, feeble one, then how much more a crime is it to rob a whole family? And as families produce nations, then what is it to rob a nation of its right to all of life?

It is a million times worse crime to give a puny existence to a human being than to take a life. People who are born have a right to a strong, robust, full life of healthful vigor, that every breath may make existence an ecstacy. If a man who kills another deserves punishment by death, what do these people deserve who rob the nation of its life?—these perpetrators, the law-makers, and we, their aiders and abettors in the crime, who look on complacently and smile? Virtue has its own reward. It is a pity this crime could not recoil upon the heads of the offenders with a thousand times greater rigor than it does on the innocent victims, our young girls. It is useless to tell an unthinking boy of ten years, that to take nothing from nothing, nothing remains. A child-girl, herself not matured, cannot produce mature offspring. Then why allow a marriage contract to cover this premature period of a girl's life, that she may be married at twelve? All laws constructed to govern and control the interests of women, and especially of girls, prove that their constructors are uneducated simpletons, devoid of an atom of honor, and ought to be called upon to step down and out, and let somebody wise enough, unaided by a suggestion from women, to legislate for us, and tell us what other element is more essential for the well-being of the nation than our motherhood; but let them be honest enough to fix the adult age of the girl and boy at exactly the same period, and not pretend to intelligent physiologists that girls mature sooner than boys. If this were true, women would die sooner, and every one knows there are more centenarians among women than men. There is no difference in the cutting and shedding of the teeth of boy-babies and girl-babies. If girls grew faster than boys they would not require so many months of gestation.

Out of what false reasoning did this absurd lie fasten its fangs upon poor humanity? It came from out the lowest, basest passions of man's nature, and that and that alone keeps it still a dominant power. It is the hot blast of beastliness that makes men legislate in this unjust manner for women. Beastliness, inasmuch as it is without reason. In any other sense it is a libel on the beast, since their animalism is a clean record when compared with that of man. Do women know that to endure all this wrong in silence makes them vile infinitely baser than the men who impose these crimes upon them, since they are the chosen handmaids of God to the highest and holiest mission on earth, that of propagating the species, the architects and builders of His people, of the world, a responsible position too holy to be injured? Women should not submit to wrong themselves and their children yet unborn. But the dawn when women will awaken to action is glowing with roseate hue. The cold, gray dull clouds are passed. Our public schools, with their millions of growing girls, equally educated with our boys, will do the work in a few years of enlightening our women to their true status in life. Education will make them grand, true, brave women. They will not ask for their rights; why should they? They will take up their duties and act their rights. They will make their own laws to govern their own persons and property. Then the nation will begin to grow, and drop its shackles. We shall be a strong, healthy, noble race, not cursed by disease, nor poverty, nor premature death. We shall be so full of happiness that there will be no room for disease in or about us. Glorious, is it not to contemplate? The grand time coming for us all — all happy, and prosperous!

CHAPTER XXI.

SAVING HER MOTHER'S LIFE.

Jean's mother had been sick two weeks. Mr. Cursica Miser had been relegated to the loft with the boys, to spend his honeymoon in his same old-bachelor bed, all alone. The house had from three to four neighbor women in it, day and night. It was the first case of serious illness that had occurred in the neighborhood, and caused general alarm. There came at this time a terrible rain-storm. All the streams, rivers, creeks and sloughs were flooded. It was impossible for the Mission doctor to get to Mrs. Murdstone, or for anyone to reach him for advice. Roads and bridges had not materialized; they were as yet the dreams of the future. There was, however, a simple-minded old nurse, that gave herb teas to the sick, who came with a long bag filled with packages of dry herbs hanging on her arm. Jean hated her the moment she saw her, and was watchful of her movements about her mother. She was a patient, meek-faced woman, who looked as though to be meek, enduring and long-suffering was all there was to do in the world. But out of this lack of resistance grew Jean's strong advantage, as she set the old lady aside and filled the position of doctor and nurse at her mother's bedside.

Jean, though a child, was a student of nature. On the plains, the year before, she had, in her method, dissected every animal that came into camp, though not very scientifically, it is true. She had taken fibers from the great bundle of sheaths that form the muscles of the buffalo bull's neck, and the fine fibers of the antelope's ham, and called her mother's attention to the fact that there were people in the company who were made of fine fiber like that of the antelope, and those composed of coarser structure like the buffalo's neck. The mother had said:

"My child, how wonderful your turn of mind is. I should never have thought of such a thing, and yet it seems true enough, and this is quite a demonstration."

If she had known that the knowledge the girl was gaining in her studies would have enabled her to set aside ignorant authority and save her life, it would have seemed to Mrs. Murdstone still more astonishing. Sometimes, Jean had hours to give to these critical examinations of the structure of animals, sometimes only moments. She would take the hunter's knife and open the intestines, closely scanning the difference between the great and the small, the strong and the weak. Sometimes, she was alone with the animal in the tall grass, searching for knowledge as for hidden treasure, but oftener had a gaping crowd about her. Nothing hindered her, however, from knowing what she wished to learn. The strong fibers she found in the wings of the birds that fly long distances gave her much food for thought.

It was evening when the great crisis came. The tallow candles were lighted, and gave to the room such a dim weird glow that the nurse seemed to Jean like something supernatural, and drove her almost to desperation. There were four or five tin cups of different kinds of herb tea sitting in a row on the hearth, that gleamed like evil spirits before the fire, and Jean felt that they were doing her mother harm. The fire-light would blaze up and disclose everything distinctly in the room, then almost die out again, seeming to Jean to say, "Your mother's life is fast flitting away."

Mrs. Murdstone was lying, white as a sheet, not a particle of color in her lips. She had had metrorrhagy for days. She called the nurse to see what was pressing on the pelvic muscles. The nurse had told Jean she was too young for her to be about her mother—it was immodest; and Jean had answered, wrathfully: "I shall leave my mother to no one." Jean became aware of the intention of the nurse to remove the obstruction. It was inversion of the uterus, and she took the nurse by the shoulders and whirled her half across the room, saying: "Oh, mother, it is a part of your own person, and must not be removed, but replaced." Whereupon Mrs. Murdstone fainted, and Jean performed the work, and saved her mother's life, and of course was greatly excited. As soon as she could leave her mother, going into the kitchen, she bolted the door, and knelt down with her head between the pots and kettles on a bench, and in that humiliating attitude took a vow that if God would only save her mother's life, before any gray hairs should gather on her head she would know how to take care of women and not be as ignorant as those she saw about her. When she rose to her feet she knew her mother would get well. What a long, long time it did take, she being like an infant, having to be fed like one. Jean was her nurse for months.

CHAPTER XXII.

THE INDIAN HUT.

Mr. Miser was becoming restive. His marriage secured to him his land claim. This bauble sufficed to divert his mind for a time, but like the average man, he soon forgot his promises made before marriage.

One morning in midwinter, the Oregon mists, all swept away, left a cloudless sky; the sun, warm and clear, shining overhead, but mud and slush and water under foot. Messrs. Murdstone and Miser, leaning against the fence, were basking in the sunshine. Jean noted the two men. She had held them well in hand during her mother's protracted and dangerous illness, but was sure some mischief was being planned, yet did not dare to say so to her mother, who continued to be in so weak a condition that not an unpleasant breath of anything must disturb her quiet. There she lay, so feeble, behind the white curtains that surrounded her bed. A faint tinge of color was creeping back into her face. Jean sat combing and dallying with her mother's long flowing hair, and was saying, "It's so soft and shiny, and hasn't a gray hair in it, mother mine," when the door opened and Mr. Miser entered. He had rarely been in the sick-room. Did he know it was his falsehood and intrigue that had caused her this attack of long illness?

He looked quizzical, remarking, "Oh, you will soon be well and about."

"I hope so," came in a thin, faint whisper from the pillows.

Mr. Miser had trouble with a tuft of hair growing on top of his head. He would run his fingers through it as if they were a comb, lifting it up and spreading it carefully on top of his head like a plaster. His vanity caused him to think that Jean's smile was a sure indication that she was pleased with his personal appearance, and dubiously returning her smile, asked, "If your mother can spare you, Jean, will you go to ride? Your pony is at the door."

"Oh, yes, mamma can spare me."

And as they moved out of the room, Mrs. Murdstone drew the curtain aside with her white hand and followed them with her eyes. Jean never forgot that look. They rode over the Murdstone place, and half the Miser estate, and halted in front of the cabin door, where Mr. Miser told Jean they were going to live. That he would put a puncheon floor over half the cabin, for a bed-room, and a dirt floor would suffice for the remainder of the cabin. He would pile up some stones against the wall, make a hole in the clapboard roof for the smoke to escape, which would take the place of a chimney. He opened a rudely constructed door made of clapboards, and together they entered the hut. Jean's heart was almost standing still, while the handsomest eyes that ever lighted a handsome face, scanned the man who had the power and right to bring her to such a place to live, and she decided that blanched cheeks or moist eyes could have no more effect upon him than they did the dirt she was standing upon. Therefore, she laughed a little pluckily, saying:

"What wonderful plans for improvement, Mr. Miser. You would make this hut a little palace."

"You must call this a cabin," he answered, in severe tones, putting his fingers through his hair, and plastering it solidly on top of his head, adding:

"I should not like the neighbors to say that we live in a hut. Such things are picked up very quickly in this new country."

And Jean with a little laugh, spiritedly replied:

"The way to prevent that is not to live in a hut,"

THE INDIAN HUT.

and she patted the mane of the chestnut sorrel that stood close to the cabin door.

They mounted again, and, riding home, Mr. Miser explained that he wished to set three or four men to work, and they must commence housekeeping at once. Jean ventured to query, "I thought you were going to build a new house, and leave me at mother's while you were getting things ready?"

"My, what a grand lady. We get things ready for you! Why, don't you know you are only a poor girl?" sneered Miser with the trickiest smile that ever disclosed villainy in a man's face.

Jean, with scorn wreathing her lips, asked: "Did you not tell my mother so?"

With the sinister smile deepening: "What would not a man tell to get a girl these hard times, when the United States government allows him the alternative to marry or be robbed of his land?"

Jean's mother was asleep when she entered. From this she knew that Mr. Murdstone had not told her anything to disturb her. This gave Jean time to bathe her face, and put back the tears that would come. She hoped it would take some weeks for Mr. Miser to make these extensive improvements. If her mother could be well again! She would do anything in her power to coax her back to health and strength. She would bend every energy while she was with her to hasten her recovery. She requested Murdstone and Miser to allow her to disclose the fact to her mother that she was going to housekeeping. She thought if she could make her mother believe that it was her desire to make the change, it would rob this parting of half its sting, and so prevent Mrs. Murdstone from being thrown into a relapse, which she much feared might occur.

On the last evening, as they sat by the fire, Jean's brother, Will Ames, hearing Mr. Miser remark that the cabin was fixed up good enough for a poor girl to live in, and being indignant at the idea of Mr. Miser's speaking thus of his sister, turned full upon him and said:

"You cut and hewed those logs when you first came home from California, to build a house for Eufamie Shrum, and you let the logs rot in the woods, when she would not have you. Now, because, as you just said, my sister is a poor girl, that old Indian hut is good enough for her to live in. I would not go one step, Jean, until he hauls those logs in and puts up as good a house as this, or as the other settlers in the neighborhood have. Everybody will laugh at you if you live in such a hut. Besides, mother's too sick for you to leave her now."

Will stood up straight as an arrow. He looked manly as these words flowed freely from his lips. Jean was proud of him. Mr. Miser twitched his sombrero a little more over his eyes, saying:

"What a champion you have in your big brother!" (he was only twelve years of age). "I shall have to be careful what I say."

Ridicule was his ever ready weapon to ward off criticism from himself.

This cabin had been built five years before by some half-breed Indians, belonging to the Hudson Bay Company, who lived in the French prairie. All Indians are clannish to a degree that will not admit of isolation, and they abandoned the cabin after it was built. They had a large herd of horses that liked the hills for their range, and they could drive them out of the hills to the valley, and often lasso three or four of the band for riding horses, turn the others loose, and immediately they took to the hills away.

The Indians seemed to know where to build their houses as instinctively as the birds do. This cabin was located in quite a romantic spot, on a little rise of ground, covered here and there with wide-spreading oaks, with now and then a stately fir. Near by, ran a babbling brook, with maple, ash, alder, pine, willow and hazel trees lining its banks. Back of the cabin sloped a gradually rising hill, farther and farther, higher and higher, until, when the sun was setting, it looked like a mountain piercing the cloudless sky. On

THE INDIAN HUT. 139

the other side of the creek, stretched a gradually undulating plain for miles away, in about the center of which stood the Murdstone dwelling and grounds, and Jean could easily see her mother's house from the cabin.

The last night that Jean was at home with her mother she sat in front of the bright blazing fire. A pile of oak logs were burning and dropping their great solid coals on the hearth, and were soon consumed into light gray ashes. How like the old home in Illinois, before Mr. Murdstone came. Oh, for those days back again. She at school, her mother sewing in her neat dress, her face glowing with perfect health, the children playing in the corner just as they were now; and if she must be married, why could it not have been to any one of the dozen schoolboys who used to be so delighted when it rained or snowed, and she allowed them to carry her umbrella—they thought her somebody—instead of that old man in the corner, with the slouched hat over his eyes, who thought her nobody because she was poor, and who no longer attempted to disguise his age by putting shoe blacking on his beard.

"Are not all children born poor?" she queried; "all born alike? Of course some have more things given to them by their families. Had he any right to twit her about what she could not help, and degrade her by taking her into an Indian hut? If I were half as smart as my brother Will, I would not go one step until the new house is built. Riches do not make a man nice, nor does it make girls nasty to be poor." Thus her thoughts smouldered like the ashes on the hearth, but at length she forgot her grief as all children do, and took part in the fun and laughter that was growing quite boisterous, as the mother was well enough to endure the noise, and the father was spending the evening at a neighbor's, for there was never a sound of laughter or merriment in the house when Murdstone was in it, and thus the fun ran riot when he was out of it. Next morning, when Jean was muffled in her warm wraps, her sweet little face clasped between her mother's white hands for the good-by kiss, her countenance glowing with intelligence, her mother thought: " Why she looks almost a woman. My poor child, this is such a cold, raw day. Do be careful not to take cold."

" Why, how can I, when there is a blazing fire on the hear—, or fire pla—; well, anyhow, a fire against the wall of the cabin? So don't fret about me. Intelligent people make themselves comfortable in any part of the globe, under any sky."

" But, my child, you have never lived on a dirt floor."

" Oh, you forget, in crossing the plains."

" Yes, there, too, we had the clean grass and the bright, fresh turf for a carpet."

" Yes, but, mother, I have a buffalo robe, and a long shaggy-haired bear skin, two wolf-skins, and brother Will has given me his otter skin that is too nice for a rug, and I am going to make a hair seat for you, and you must get well and come soon to see how nice it is. We have not a chair in the cabin." Here she turned and ran out of the house in a great hurry. The children were all at the gate, and clambering into the old covered wagon, hugged and kissed Jean good-bye. Miser took them all out again.

Jean thought her heart would burst. She was alone in the old wagon in which they had crossed the plains. But there, there was enjoyment, merriment, every day exciting scenes, and amusing incidents. Now some great all-absorbing terror seized her, and seemed, like midnight darkness, to envelop her as she sat there all alone. Was it a presentiment of the life she was to endure? She never could look back upon that comfortless hour's ride, with its soul torture, but a tremor would seize her. She had been busy thinking of others, but now she was alone with her own soul and her pitiable plight. She felt like one about to undergo a surgical operation where great suffering is to be endured, and life itself endangered; like one man going to battle without drum, fife, flag, or comrade, not even a canteen of cold water. She longed

THE INDIAN HUT.

to hear the sound of voices; she wished her husband to speak to her. He walked silently beside the dumb cattle; only the death-like stillness reigned. She tried to think how she would arrange her household. She could think of nothing but this nameless horror. What was it? Was her mother dying, she soliloquized? If all the friends she had ever known were already dead, she could not feel worse.

They are at the cabin. Mr. Miser pulls a buckskin string, and the clapboard door swings back with an ominous creaking on its wooden hinges; and the old wood rat that had made its nest in the corner, the squirrels that are frisking over the roof, the blue-jay that is digging out some of the acorns that he laid away for his winter use, all scamper and fly the invasion. An old crow sits on a long pole that projects from the roof, caw, caw, cawing. Jean calls it the bird of ill-omen, throws a stone at him, and away he flies. The bugs and worms, and the old hanging bark that had broken loose from the logs, and hangs in shreds all over the cabin, a hiding-place for the bugs and worms —these and the dust, the bloom of time, remain. Jean had already determined in her own mind to entertain no friendly relations with the present occupants of the cabin.

CHAPTER XXIII.

THEY WERE NOT THE BUGS OF CIVILIZATION.

Jean's mother, with the consent of Mr. Murdstone, had loaned her one of the wagon covers to make a house lining in the corner of the cabin where the bed was to stand. This would serve as a protection to the sleepers from the strongest draft of wind, and also prevent the keen-eyed savages from peering in; but more than all, prevent the easy access to the bed, of the bugs, worms and spiders whose hiding place was behind the dead bark of the logs that composed the cabin. She fastened a tester sheet to this lining at the back and head of the bed. In front, and at the foot of the bed, she fastened drapery of well-ironed sheets, whose snowy folds fell nearly to the floor. Around the bottom of the bedstead she placed a valance of blue and white broad-checked gingham, which was a shiny accessory to the bed, and looked almost as much out of place in the cabin as she herself. When she had made the bed, with its snowy sheets and plump pillows, it looked good enough for a palace. The bedstead was made of Oregon curly maple, by a cabinet-maker, and given her by her mother—the only real piece of furniture in the hut.

Mr. Miser said, "It looks charming now, but after a few gusts of smoke from my patent fire-place it will present a very different appearance."

Jean replied, "The curtains will protect the bed, and they can be washed semi-occasionally."

Mr. Miser had utilized some of the puncheon boards to construct a table, by putting the ends of the boards through the crack between the logs of the cabin, and two legs and a cross-piece to hold up the front of the table. Jean covered it with a snowy tablecloth, and set a very comfortable meal that she had brought cooked, from her mothers'. The table was solid, but rougher than a storm at sea. The fire was burning cheerfully, and the smoke curling out of the hole in the roof, to her great surprise; but she thought to herself, "As God tempers the wind to the shorn lamb, so he is adapting the wind to the chimney." How she missed that quiet composure that pervaded her home when they all sat around the table, waiting for the blessing to be asked. The meal being over, she busied herself clearing away the dishes, arranging them on their little clapboard shelves, that Mr. Miser had fastened to the wall, and called a cupboard. She took a kitchen apron which she fastened to the back of the shelves, and at the front of these rough boards she tacked some narrow ruffling, then she set away the few pieces of crockery, tin cups and plates; the knives, forks and spoons she put in a covered box, and all the food in the iron bake-kettle for security. By deft and shrewd management, constant and eternal vigilance, she kept herself from being eaten or eating any of the bugs, worms or spiders that inhabited the hut along with herself and husband.

These were not, dear reader, the bugs of civilization, known as the bed-bug, nor the festive flea, nor the musical mosquito. They were bugs indigenous to that particular climate and hut. They belonged to the half-decayed fir log. They were a species that did not take long ranges from their native habitat. The little housekeeper, however, not understanding their peculiar traits of character, and being shocked at the thought of any closer companionship with them, barricaded against them with might and main. Miser had made two rude benches from logs split in two. One, about five feet long, served him as a lounge; the other was Jean's chair, not very restful to be sure. When the life is taken out of one's soul, the body tires quickly. Next morning, after a simple breakfast, Mr.

Miser said to Jean. "I am going to Mill Creek to drive up some cattle to slaughter a beef."

Jean looked beseechingly at him, asking:

"Will you be gone all day? Then I will go to mother's, because I can't stay in this place all day alone, I am afraid," and her lip began to quiver.

"There's going to be no tagging between you and the Murdstone brats," said he, glowering upon her. "You stay right here, and bake some bread; nothing will hurt you. There will be four men here to-night for supper. They are going to work on the ranch. Two will go to plowing, and two will go into the woods to chop down trees, and hew logs to build your ladyship a house to live in. You d— fool, do you think (with more oaths), that the trees will chop themselves down and walk out of the woods on to this lovely ground, and make themselves into a beautiful residence for you, because you are a mighty lady?"

At the first volley of oaths Jean put her apron up to her face, her slight frame trembling with fear and horror, the tears falling like rain. She stopped crying, saying:

"I must go to see my mother to-day."

"You'll not go one step; but stay at home and make bread, and, while it is baking, you can read in your Bible that nice little story about Lot and his daughters, and how David, the man after God's own heart, took Uriah's wife to himself to wife."

Then he mounted his pony with a great flourish, half singing:

"Hey, ho, here we go, riding on a rainbow, under a cloud, leaving a rain-storm behind."

No Indian could have looked wilder, with his slouched hat flying in the wind, then he did, as Jean heard his horse's clattering hoofs, and saw him, through her tears, galloping away.

Jean did not believe there were any such stories in the Bible. She put her head on the table and cried until she could scarcely see. She bolted the cabin-door, as they had done the previous evening, then crawled behind the curtains into her bed, more dejected and miserable than any worm behind the old dead bark in the logs that made her wretched prison cell and theirs.

Jean had heard men swear on the plains when they were very angry, but she thought them the offscourings of the earth; they were not people with whom her family would associate, any member of which would have been guilty of any crime as soon as swearing or lying. She learned, alas! so soon that Mr. Miser cared no more whether his word fell on the side of truth or falsehood, than the wind cares whether it blows to the north or the south. If her mother had been well she would have flown home to her. But as she was too sick to hear a wail from her, she would obey her husband, bake the bread, and try so hard to be a woman. She had thought, before her marriage, that she would love her husband like other women; when she grew to be a woman, she would be a model wife. Although her head was aching ready to burst, she thought she would get up and bake the bread and have the evening meal prepared for the hired men when they came, and trying to stand on her feet she grew so sick she thought she was dying, and fell back on the bed. Life's voyage was making her sea-sick as a storm at sea; and she lay all day so limp and lifeless, not caring if the ship with its living freight sunk to the bottom of the sea, just as you and I, dear reader, have felt a thousand times when very sick at sea. About three o'clock in the afternoon, she heard a noise like the surging sound of mighty waters, then the tread of horses' hoofs, then the lowing of cattle, and the hallooing of men, and raising her head from the pillow, the excitement together with the exertion of rising made the rebellious contents of her stomach eject themselves upon the puncheon floor. Just at this moment Mr. Miser opened the cabin door. She looked so white he thought for a moment she might be dying, and with some show of alarm, brought her a tin cup of cold water. She could not drink it. It was not fresh from the spring. He coolly remarked: "That d—— crying made you sick," and left her, to give directions about killing the beef.

They gave the herd salt to eat on the ground, and as they were licking away at the salt, all unmindful of the deadly bullet that the man let fly with well-directed aim, one animal fell to rise no more, and now the loud bellowing of the herd as they smelled the fresh blood flowing from their comrade's wound was enough to make a heart of stone ache, yet Jean had to hear it all, so near. She lay in her bed so sick, so thankful for the screen of curtains that hid her from the view of those rough men. Miser brought a hired man of nineteen into the cabin, who, after he had shown him the cooking utensils, rolled up his sleeves, and very soon announced to the slaughterers that he was ready for the beefsteak. They yelled back: "You are a daisy; got supper in a jiffy."

They brought some huge slices of the meat that was still warm, put it into the frying pan, where it fried up quickly, then sat down to partake of a meal of this delicious steak, with hot biscuit, and hot potatoes, boiled with their jackets on. They drank their coffee out of the bright tin cups, and were awed into silence by the neatness of their surroundings. They knew the sick woman, hid from their view, was one of refinement and delicacy. Their respectful consideration was very soothing to the sufferer. The tension of fear taken off her nerves was fast relieving her head of its acute pain. Her brother Will came at sundown, and rode his horse's nose right into the cabin door. The horse, thinking it a shabby stable, was about to walk in. This brought a laugh both within and without the cabin. Jean, hearing the clatter, pulled the curtain aside, and Will, getting a glimpse of Jean lying there, slid from the horse, and in an instant clasped her to his breast, saying:

"My poor sister, are you sick?" and their tears mingled together.

"Oh, Will, why did you not come sooner?" wailed Jean, her slight frame trembling in her brother's arms.

That morning, when Will was driving up the milk cows from the pasture, he espied, down by the low, murmuring brook, first by the fragrance and then by the bloom, a little full-blown primrose on a bush glistening with dew, like diamond drops, all studded with buds half bursting. "This was a beauty," he said to Jean as he took it out of his pocket, all crushed and bruised, "my dear sis, the sweet little thing was just like you when I picked it this morning, all shining with dew;" and Jean took it smiling. "It is more like me now, all crushed with this headache," and she took a deep breath, inhaling the delicious fragrance. "A smell, brother, will kill or cure me sooner than anything." Then she told him how the old wood-rat had been walking about all day, with such a stinking nasty smell. It had been investigating things, and had poked its nose against the bake-oven lid a dozen times. Once it frightened her almost to death by trying to run up the curtain. She threw her shoe at it, and it scampered away. But the blue jays came and twittered and pecked, and pecked and twittered again, eating the acorns out of the logs on the cabin roof where they had hidden them for their winter's use. And the old crow, that she threw a stone at yesterday—was it only yesterday? and the tears glistened in her eyes as she said it—came back with a dozen others. "They must have been talking about our coming in here, I think, by the dignified way they walked back and forth over the shingles, caw, caw, cawing and making remarks, some of them not very flattering, I should think from the sound, to the people who would take an old crow's rookery like this to live in." The two children continued talking until the men had gone out to work, when Will brought his sister some coffee with some sweet cream, that he had carried in a bottle from his mother's. She drank it, and ate a mouthful of bread, feeling very much revived. Next morning, Will came again, asking for Jean to return to her mother's for a few days. Miser consented, saying: "She is only an expense here and not worth a d——." So the children went rejoicing on their homeward way.

Jean spent one blessed week in the old home; then back again to her prison pen and slavery for six months in the hut. Just imagine the horror of sitting on that old bench on the dirt floor, afraid the bugs would crawl from the ground to her feet and dress, or that they might at any moment drop into her hair from the rough roof, and then the eternal vigilance, that forever listening attitude, born of fear, that the murderous savages might surprise her by slipping up in their moccasined feet, over the soft turf, still as death, and tomahawking her without an instant's warning.

Was ever the felon's cell equal to this? Talk of the Bastile; criticise foreign countries for their tyrannies to the people; the Czar of Russia for his cruelties to the exiles; and deluge the nation in blood to free a handful of negro slaves, when an hour's cool-headed legislation would have freed them and did free them at last, and without which they would not have been freed had they fought till now, and then take your brightest and best American girl-children, and make their lives like this. Flaunt your flags, and shoot your guns, and talk of Fourth of July. The great American nation, free under the American flag.

This child had a right under the constitution of our beloved country, to the pursuit of happiness. Do not forget that it was the laws of our beloved country that exiled this girl-child from her home, and forged the chains that held her in that prison pen, and do not forget also, my brainy reader, that it was the acumen of the greatest minds that our boasted civilization has yet produced that formulated these laws. Let us help you further to remember that this condition of things did not grow out of the scum, the festering ulcer, the hot-bed of our evil-doers, the poor and uneducated, the lower classes, but from the highest element; the wise, the learned, the god-like, the good; they that feel proud of the intellectual heights they have attained. We wish to inflate them still more by showing them how their edicts in law, work out a problem in human life, by showing them this one. Give us an extra strut, gentlemen, when you walk the earth, god-like mortals; and lift your hats a little higher, never catching a glimpse of the contempt, the lip wreathed in scorn, of the beautiful woman you have passed. And get an idea, you quick-witted readers that the life of the one little child we are trying to give you a glimpse of, is only one of thousands who are imprisoned just the same, whose lives may be, in some respects better, in many, infinitely worse. We have very tender consideration for your lack of comprehension, brother man, your muddled brain, your supreme ignorance of everything that is essential for you to know before you legislate for girl-children; and therefore we make the question simple, so that even you, oh man, may comprehend it. If it requires twenty-one years for a man to mature sufficiently to cast a vote intelligently for the purpose of securing office for some simpleton, would it not require an equal amount of intellectual maturity to select a helpmeet for life? As men and women are equal, then should not both arrive at the age of twenty-one years, before they be allowed by the laws of the land to be united in marriage?

CHAPTER XXIV.

JEAN'S HOME SOLD WITHOUT HER CONSENT.

At last the new house was completed, with its shingle roof, sawed lumber, roughly planed for a floor, two doors, and an old-fashioned window with panes of glass ten by twelve inches, a broad porch stretching away on either side of the front door. A broad fire-place, built of rough stone and clay, with its wide hearth of flat stone, with many a crack here and there, that taxed Jean's energy to the utmost to keep free from dirt and ashes. Mr. Miser's peculiar disposition to hoard his gold had now become so apparent to Jean that she knew that he was in every way a Miser—both in name and nature. To her astonishment, he told her that the things that were in the old house would do for the new, and did not add even a chair. But the house was so clean and so secure that she felt like one of the spirits of the damned that had been confined in Hades, and was now lifted to Heaven, the change from dirt to cleanliness was so great. Jean lived in this broad, spacious, one-roomed house in comparative comfort for a year and a half. She had become accustomed to Miser's one peculiar phrase that she had not as much sense as a "yaller dog." He was so constantly planning villainy against his neighbors, that he did not dare to speak before Jean for fear of disclosing his plans. When he entered the house, it was his habitual custom to hang his hat on a peg, put his fingers through his hair, and, with the remark that his "nerves were shottered," lie down on the bench, one hand under his head for a pillow, the other shading his eyes. This was his attitude during every moment spent in the house. Any woman who has passed through the perils of maternity must know how Jean longed for a little sympathy as her time of trial drew near—a little tenderness. It never came in word or look. After three days of agony, at the very verge of death, after praying that she might never breathe again, and thus be relieved of this terrible torture, she lay for weeks before she was conscious that a little puny life—a feeble, wailing thing—was by her side, and that her mother was hovering over her with the tears falling like rain in the blessed joy that Jean knew her again. All the bitter protests of Mr. Murdstone, and all the oaths of Mr. Miser, could not wrench Jean's mother from her side. She said she required her care to bring her back to life, and she and the little one received her watchful solicitude for three months. And when Mr. Miser said he wished Jean and the baby were both dead and out of the way, some words escaped Mrs. Murdstone's lips that she thought afterwards she should not have spoken. They were the dawning of truth and justice in her mind. She did not recognize them as such. They were these: "If Jean were at home again, she should remain there until she was a woman." Will Ames, with rebellion in his heart, said, "It's a shame! They are two babies together.' And Jean's soul was riveted to his, though she lay there so helpless. Her first conscious grief, after returning to life, was that Mr. Miser never came near nor looked at the baby, and her next great disappointment was that a pleasant morning caller apprized her of the fact that her home was sold and she was to move one hundred and fifty miles from her mother and her present home—no family living within fifty miles of the new habitation. Jean hated the woman for the news, and quoted to her mother, "How beautiful upon the mountain top are the feet of him that bringeth glad tidings." And when she questioned Mr. Miser about it, he answered, with one of his foxy smiles, that he knew nothing about it, and if it were true, she would find it out soon enough. And Jean answered, "You can sell your land, but I'll not sell mine. We have gone through too many hardships to secure the land."

It was the Methodist missionary, the Rev. Mr. William Roberts, a gentleman much more noted for his suavity of manner and duplicity of character than for his religious teachings, who contrived with Mr. Cursica Miser to rob Jean of her land, her home near her mother that she had paid dearly for. Old Shylock's pound of flesh wasn't a flea-bite compared with what Jean was paying. The reverend gentleman and the defrauding husband had written to the Land Department at Washington to have the title of the land made out in the name of Mr. Roberts and his wife.

As Jean signed the deed, which she blotted with her tears, and the glittering gold was counted out, and laid upon the table by the reverend gentleman, she said, sorrowfully, "The cursed gold that cost me this!"

If she had been a woman, instead of wiping the tears from her eyes, she would have wiped the reverend gentleman out of the house, and never signed the paper. But as it was, Mr. Miser damned her fluently for crying and setting the neighbors to jibing him, and saying, as he termed it, that he had "swindled her out of her land."

And Jean asked, half smiling, "Is it my tears and not your acts that cause the neighbors to say this? I think they say the truth."

"We will go where we have no neighbors," snapped the enterprising Mr. Miser, adding his usual number of adjectives. And they did.

Jean's baby boy, who was now a year and a half old, was the joy of her existence. She and her mother had begged Mr. Miser to go on horseback to select his government land, but he insisted upon Jean's going in the ox-wagon and coming back again. It took them six weeks to make the trip. Theirs were the first wagon-wheels that passed over the government road that fighting Joe Hooker, in the summer of 1851, had surveyed for the government through Oregon to California, and had marked the road by a furrow plowed to indicate the line of the survey all the way through the Willamette Valley until he reached the

Umpqua mountains, where he chipped the trees to mark the route. In all this vast expanse of country, the broad valleys, rolling hills, towering mountains and rough woodland, there were located but two families, one at Spalding's Ferry, where Eugene City sits like a fair diadem crowning the valley, and the other the Applegate family, where Yoncolla now nestles between the thickly studded hills. Mr. Miser called a halt on the North Umpqua river, fifteen miles above where Roseburg is now located.

Three white men had preceded the Misers, with a small band of Indian ponies, that rumor said they had driven away from the California ranches without the ceremony of a permit from their former owners. The Indians, who had never seen a white woman before, appeared to be very friendly. Jean was almost as terrorized by their friendly attentions as she would have been at their hostility. They crowded around her, every one of the band touching her dress, some of the matronly old savages even patted her shoulders and smoothed down her soft dark tresses. They took the comb out of her brown hair, letting it fall down in heavy ripples, and as it fell their tongues began to clatter with the greatest enthusiasm. Jean wondered if they were planning to take her beautiful scalp as a trophy. "Hyou typso," went from mouth to mouth, which she afterwards learned meant great quantity of hair.

The soft liquid sounds "sappalilli, sappalilli," fell on her ears in a chorus of voices. This meant to convey the idea that they were rejoiced at the coming of the whites, as now they would have bread. Though the white men said there was no danger of an attack from the Indians, yet they took the precaution to build a little log pen inside their cabin, wherein they could securely sleep at night, and where Indian arrows could not reach them. Cursica Miser located a claim of six hundred and forty acres of land on the banks of the Umpqua, where the wild grasses grew luxuriantly on the river bottom, shooting their tasselated spears above a man's hat when on horseback. After a few days they wended their slow way back through the Williamette Valley to the place where the capital of the great state of Oregon now flourishes. Here Jean was with her mother again for a few short weeks. It was apparent to herself and her mother that Jean's young life was again to be taxed by the perils of maternity. Her experiences had not been such, when alone with her husband, so far from any vestige of civilization, that she was eagerly desirous of having them repeated. Once during this journey they had lost their way from the main track, and were compelled to go through a heavy forest, a gloomy and melancholy place, when Jean asked Mr. Miser, "Why did you take this way instead of the way we came?" He answered, with a look of stealthy exultation, "I came this way to kill you and throw you under a tree. I would not have dragged this wagon all this long distance and back again, only for revenge for your making the row about signing the deed to the land."

Very indiscreetly Jean retorted. "Had I known you then as I know you now, I would never have signed the paper;" and her tears mingled with those of the baby whose little life was being made a torture by the dust and heat, the fatigue and thirst. The more they cried, the more the malicious grin expanded on the countenance of Cursica Miser, who repeatedly announed to Jean on this trip that he wished that she and her brat were both dead and in hell, from which language one might easily infer that the gentleman was not enjoying his revenge as much as he might have anticipated. Sitting humped up on the front seat of the wagon, his slouched hat pulled over his face, or trudging slowly along beside the dumb brutes that could scarcely crawl, over three hundred miles of rough road, under a scorching sun, could not have proved a very sweet morsel of revenge, even to one of so vindictive a nature as Mr. Cursica Miser.

Mrs. Murdstone implored Mr. Miser to leave Jean with her, assuring him that one so young and in so delicate a condition might be a source of great expense as well as inconvenience, and he, with his habitual malicious grin, acquiesced in Mrs. Murdstone's request; but in a few weeks, when the teams were all ready to start, a band of horses and cattle already moving out on the trail, Mr. Miser ordered Jean very unceremoniously to come right along with him. What could she do, but with fear and trembling obey her kind-hearted and considerate lord and master?

The writer would be glad if one of the wise persons who think that girl-children mature faster than boys, could have stood in Jean's shoes that day. Her mother stood like a stone, without tears on her face, as she clasped Jean to her breast, and thought her heart would burst.

Miser on this journey was in a measure deprived of his opportunities of perpetrating his cruel speeches upon his defenseless wife, since two hired men bore them company, one of them driving the team in which Jean and the baby rode. On account of some delays, they were fifteen days on the journey before they reached the banks of the Umpqua, where their land claim and the wide world lay spread out before them.

They soon erected an impromptu shelter of "such material as around the workman's hand most readily found." It was a lodge of ample size, eighteen by twenty feet, of a rough and rude construction, having one door for entrance, no floor, no window, no fire-place. They brought with them a cook-stove and a few chairs, and Jean her Bible and hymn-book, and a little old-fashioned dictionary. After they were settled here three or four days, Mr. Miser returning in the evening after a long tramp over the mountains and hills, investigating the amount and quality of the range they would afford for his stock, he brought with him a boy, a veritable little ruffian, Jean thought, who, Mr. Miser informed her, would remain with her and the baby in the cabin while he and the men returned to the Willamette Valley to drive back a drove of cattle that he intended to buy with the money they had realized from the sale of their home. Jean fell on her knees with an entreaty to be taken to the Applegates to remain until his return, imploring not to be left alone with the wild savages about her, who had come every day since their arrival to look at her and beg for bread. He was no more moved by her pleading than was the ground on which she knelt, but looked down upon her with the same treacherous grin, putting his fingers through his hair, and saying:

"If the Indians kill you I will gain two points; I will be rid of you, and, as the Indians will then be killed by the whites, I will be freed from their disturbing my cattle, which they will kill more or less, until they are all exterminated by us whites. I like to see you weep; you look Madonna-like with your prayers and tears."

CHAPTER XXV.

INDIANS TAKING POSSESSION.

Thus Jean was left to the mercy of the savages for six long weeks, alone with the twelve-year-old boy, nearly as wild as the Indians themselves, who roamed at their own sweet will through her cabin and out again. Sometimes the old squaws told her, as best they could, that they were sorry for her. On one occasion, when the valley tribes had been visiting with their mountain friends, hunting and fishing, their visit had terminated in a fight, which often happens in more civilized communities when people go for summer outings. The valley tribe, on their homeward march, stopped at Jean's unprotected cabin to have their wounds dressed, recruit a bit, and tie up the rents in their garments with strings. One of the squaws told Jean to give her a needle and thread, and she would sew her torn calico dress as the white squaws did theirs. They rode their ponies' noses into the cabin door. There were about thirty in all, who dismounted and walked in themselves. They were greatly excited, and talked violently to each other. Jean thought her time had come; she knew she was to be killed. The fact was certain as though the tomahawk was already buried in her brain. She knelt down in the farthest corner of the cabin, and put her apron over the child, thinking the savages might not see it if thus concealed.

The old chief, Nezic, struck with her prayerful attitude and her pale face, pounded on the door with his clenched hand to attract her attention. If he had moved toward her, she would have died with fright, but she looked up and saw the tears were streaming down his bronzed face. And putting his hand over the region of his heart, he said, "No bad tum tum" (meaning heart), and explained that he was the same as a white man, and lived in a house at the Applegates'. Jean, hearing the name of 'Applegate,' felt safe, and rousing herself rose to her feet, to show that she understood the chief, who could speak a few words of English, having lived at the Applegates' a number of years. He told Jean he would protect her from the rest of the Indians, who had taken advantage of her being alone and swarmed into her house; and at his command they all filed out, giving a grunt of dissatisfaction and a sneer of contempt, as an Indian knows well how to do. Jean immediately sent the boy on the fast steed that she kept tied at her camp, to cross the river at a very dangerous ford a mile and a half away, to tell the three men who lived on the other side of the river to come to her assistance.

The last faint sound of the flying hoofs of the messenger had scarcely been lost, when her strained ear caught the sound of the hurrying squadron of the four horsemen returning. As soon as they flung themselves from their panting steeds, and listened to Jean's story, they assured her there was no danger. Jack Smith, a man of some learning and refinement, observing her condition, soothed and attended her like a brother. He told her to go and lie down, and he would hold the Indians in check, apprehending that the fright might bring on some disastrous results that would be a little more difficult for him to control than even these wild, hostile savages. He requested the Indians to remove their camp a little farther from the cabin. They had built a fire of stove-wood not six feet from the door, and laughed at him, saying they would build their fires in their own country, of their own wood, just where they pleased, and jeeringly remarked that the pale-faced squaw should have more "tillicums," which meant "friends," and that there never was a tribe of Indians that would leave one of their squaws among the whites as this white woman was left among them.

Putting his hand over the region of his heart, he said, "No bad tum tum."

That Mr. Miser had gone to bring cattle to eat their
grass, and when he returned they would eat beef, just
as they were using his wood now; saying which, one of
them picked up a load of wood and piled it on a blazing fire near the cabin, to show Mr. Jack Smith that
they would do what they chose with their own. Mr.
Jack Smith was somewhat stung by the taunt of this
imperious squaw, Alillo, whose eyes were like an eagle's,
and her hair like the raven's wing, an olive-brown
skin, and teeth of pearl that gleamed as she thus truthfully said that no tribe of Indians would treat one of
their women as the whites did Jean. It rankled in his
breast, and on Mr. Miser's return he supposed he
would bring at least a companion and nurse for his
wife; but as there was nothing of the kind, nor could
one be obtained within a hundred miles, and, thinking
he himself would be brought into requisition, as he had
been before, to protect her from the savages, he rode
over to Miser's camp one day, and attacked that gentleman with these questions:

"I called to see in what way you expected to obtain
medical aid or assistance for your wife, Mr. Miser?
You may think it is an impertinent question, but as
you left her here alone this summer, and as we three
white men were the first to make this settlement, we
feel called upon to maintain law and order." And, with
his hand on his revolver: "We have decided that if
you neglect your wife in this shameful way, and anything happens to her, we will hang you to that
oak tree," pointing to a broad-spreading oak with low
limbs, ten feet away. "I would suggest the propriety
of your taking her back to her mother before the rains
set in."

And Cursica Miser, who was a miserable coward,
when cornered, assured Mr. Smith, with all the suavity
at his command, that he would; and that afternoon
when he came into the cabin, he made the air blue
with his oaths, and Jean never divined the cause, as
she did not understand his profane language. He
said the next time he moved he would go a hundred

miles, but he would get away from meddlesome neighbors. And in a few days Miser informed Jean that he was going to the Willamette Valley to procure a few varieties of fruit trees and some choice seeds, and that she could accompany him to her mother's and remain there during the winter. She had been dragged back and forth so often that the trip had lost its charm, if it ever had any; and when he told her that she would ride the old bay that stood fifteen hands high, and had great swaying pendulum strides like a camel on the desert, she was sure she had not the strength to take the trip, and told him so, saying:

"How will the baby go?"

"Why," said Miser, "we'll carry him as the squaws do their papooses. They travel everywhere with their children on horseback."

"Oh, it will kill him to go one hundred and fifty miles. The rains are coming, and it is so cold. Oh, why did you bring me here?"

"I brought you here for revenge for not wanting to sign that deed, and every trip you have taken this summer has been for revenge. I'll teach your ladyship not to oppose me in anything I want to do. I marry a poor girl like you, and you set yourself to rule!" And with one of the most malicious grins ever seen on his face, he concluded this tirade with, "You would not at least have been in your present helpless condition only for my revenge."

An idea was just dawning upon the soul of Jean of the evil, designing nature of her husband, and with apparently renewed strength, she answered him, bravely:

"Squaws don't have physicians, and white women have borne children in the mountains, and what others have endured, I can, and I don't want to undertake this long journey in this inclement season."

"Just because you don't want to take the journey is the very reason you shall. What do you know about it. You haven't half as much sense as a yaller dog!"

This convinced Jean that her words were useless, and her tears unavailing.

CHAPTER XXVI.

THE BRAVERY OF ALILLO, THE SQUAW.

On the afternoon of November 4th, 1852, they started on their long ride. Jack Smith came to see them off, and, helping Jean on to her horse, said, "We are only a lot of coarse, rough men, no better than the heathen, and don't know how to take care of you, so the best place for you is with your mother." He rode with them for a short distance, carrying the baby, which was now twenty months old, and grew very tired, even in that short ride, and, turning back, with a few cheering words, bade them good-by. Kindly instructing Jean not to carry him a foot of the way, he handed the baby back to Miser, saying she would have enough to to do to care for herself. They traveled a few miles down the east side of the Umpqua River, when they came to the roughest country that ever the eye of man rested upon. High mountain gorges and deep ravines; crag after crag reached to frowning battlements, and one precipice after another yawned on either side; towering mountains loomed to the right of them; the river went surging and foaming and dashing over the rocks below them. After they had gone only a few miles, Jean was gazing in awe at this wild grandeur, when suddenly her horse stopped, his form trembling beneath her, his nostrils distended, showing in every movement a protest and a determination to go no farther over the trail; and no wonder, for there was a rocky point, jutting out over the boiling abyss that lay a thousand feet below them. There was no path worn around this solid rock. It reared its towering front almost to the sky. Little Indian ponies had gone around for ages possibly, until they had worn their footprints, little cup-places, in the solid rock; but this great, tall animal on which Jean sat could not adapt its footsteps to the worn tracks of the Indian ponies. Miser had alighted, sent his horse and the pack-animal ahead, and stood there holding the baby in his arms and Jean's horse by the bridle, encouraging it to walk on. The horse had mildly but firmly protested. Jean begged to be lifted down and allowed to walk over the dangerous trail. Miser, still holding the bridle, said with an oath, "You stay where you are!" She could not slide down from the horse, as her feet hung over the precipice. The boiling torrent lay so far beneath her, she could hardly see its seething, only hear its terrible roar. Miser pulled the bridle, the animal moved a few steps, trembling more and more. Jean called, "Help me, I am fainting!" In a little crevice of the rock a chapparal bush grew. She caught at it and fell senseless on the upper side of the horse, and was thus wedged in between the horse and the side of the stone precipice. Miser, watching his own footsteps, and not knowing that Jean had fallen, continued moving on. Jean, being unconscious, had fallen six feet below, and caught on a dwarfed pine tree that had struggled into existence, to all appearances, out of the rock, wherein its roots must have penetrated and found soil to nourish it. The horse being now over this perilous place, Miser glanced around, and to his horror, discovered Jean lying against the tree. He did not dare to go to her assistance. He was a coward, and could almost feel Jack Smith's rope around his neck that moment. He hastily seized a rope, and tied the baby to a bush to save it from falling over the precipice. He tore off his hat and coat to lighten his load, mounted his horse and dashed down the mountains to an old Indian camp, a half a mile away. He screamed in stentorian tones for assistance. The same squaw,

THE BRAVERY OF ALILLO.

Alillo, that had taunted Jack Smith, was there. She could understand a little of the English language. She mounted her pony, told the Indians to follow, and in ten minutes was bending over Jean, afraid that the slender tree would give way and let them both down. She tore off her buckskin belt and fastened it around the tree. By this time an Indian was on the rock above her, who threw her a lariat which she tied securely to the belt on the tree, three Indians holding it tightly at the upper end. Supported by this rope, she lifted Jean's still unconscious form and pushed it up against the almost perpendicular rock, until the Indian men could reach her dress. They carried her around the precipice, and laid her down beside the baby, whose screams ought to have waked the dead. They thought Jean dead. Alillo chafed her hands, and blew into her face; she sighed, and her eyes opened upon the same brave Alillo, her face lit up with so much benevolence, bending over her with as much solicitude as her own mother could have done. She carried Jean down to the Indian camp, and nursed her tenderly for days. Next day Jean lay so still on her fern couch that Alillo had picked fresh for her, and which smelled so sweet and fragrant it seemed like a couch of down to her. She was compelled to lie so still, as she was threatened with premonitory symptoms of a very serious character. Alillo was by her side, bringing little dainty morsels to eat, or a slice of salmon trout, which grow about a foot long, and are the finest fish that ever swam in water; this she would split in two, and put on a forked stick placed before a blazing wood fire, where soon it would be a delicious brown. Then she would bring it to Jean, with a loaf of snowy bread, that Jean had baked before leaving home, and the two squaws, the white and the dusky brown, sat and ate and chatted, and became well acquainted with each other's different countries, and people, and their methods of living. It was remarkable how, through a bond of sympathy, these two women could understand each other's most profound philosophies, religions, and customs, when neither of them could comprehend but a few words of the other's language.

Alillo asked, "What was your first thought when you opened your eyes and saw me bending over you when you had fainted?"

"I knew nothing of the great danger I had passed through," replied Jean. "I knew nothing of your risking your life to deliver me from that most perilous position. I knew the Great Spirit had saved me. I felt my head resting on a stone. The sun was setting. It seemed a great way below us—so beautiful—the whole sky bathed in a soft roseate glow. It seemed like heaven, and so near we could almost drop into it, and the words of the poet seemed a part of my being: "Though like a wanderer, my rest a stone. Nearer, my God to Thee, nearer to Thee."

An Indian messenger was sent to Jack Smith, who came riding into camp. The Indians, who, strange to say, send their messages over hill and valley, mountain and dale, almost as quickly as we send our telegraphic communications, brought the tidings to Jack Smith, the night that this accident occurred, and he was in the camp early the next morning, and helped them over to the Applegate settlement, accompanied by Alillo and several other Indians. When Smith asked Miser why he allowed his wife to ride over that dangerous place, Miser whined that he tried to persuade her to alight from her horse, but she refused to obey, and Jean was too much afraid to tell him the truth. If she had, Jack Smith would never have left her till he had seen her safe in her mother's house, in her mother's arms. Nothing could have been more tender, solicitous or kind than the Applegate women were to Jean, and yet she was almost ashamed to acknowledge to herself that she did not feel that warm glow of friendship between herself and the Applegate women that she did for this wild, untutored, savage Alillo. She doubted if one of these white women, if put to the test, would have risked her life for her as Alillo had. She told Alillo so, and also that her people should be befriended by the

whites when it was in her power to influence them.
Alillo returned Jean the graceful compliment, that she
knew Jean must be very influential with the great men
of her nation.

Jean, being unconscious, had fallen.

CHAPTER XXVII.

THREE DAYS' RAINY RIDE.

After parting with Alillo and Jack Smith, and the Indians that had followed in their wake as companions, Mr. Miser, Jean and the baby commenced the ascent of the Calaypooa Mountains, reaching the summit about sundown on the same day. Halting, they made a blazing camp-fire beside an old dead log. The air was cold and piercing, as there had been a light flurry of snow, covering the bushes and boughs of the trees; but, as the ground was warm, the snow melted as soon as it fell, making it very wet and sloppy. Jean's horse very often slipped, and once or twice fell to its knees, jarring her very seriously, making her tired and lame in every joint. She could neither sit nor stand after alighting from the horse and pillowing her head on the friendly root of an old fir tree, where she rested till Mr. Miser brought her coffee, which, with a few mouthfuls of bread, revived her, and she sat gazing on the wild, weird place, too tired to care if the wolves and bears came and devoured them all. That night she slept on the hard, cold ground, with only the blankets between her and cold mother earth. The marvelous beauty of the bedchamber was enchanting, but she lay there too exhausted scarcely to note its beauty. The snow glistening on the broad leaves of the underbrush, the lace-like fringe that the fir-tree boughs made with their white cover; the stars that shone where she could peep through and see a bit of the heavens; the tall spires of the dark trees piercing the dome above her, gave a charm and grandeur to the wild scene that could not well be surpassed.

When she awoke next morning the sun shone brightly here and there in patches where it could reach through the timber. She found the ascent much more gradual and less fatiguing. At last they reached the head of the Willamette Valley, and traveled several miles over it, before striking camp that night. Jean took heart, feeling that the worst of the journey was past, and they went to bed under the open sky, on the soft grass. In the night she felt the rain-drops falling on her face, and knew it was raining. She covered her face with her blanket, nestled her baby more closely to her form, and went on sleeping soundly. When she awoke in the morning she found it pouring rain, and her blanket floating in a pool of water. Mr. Miser was up, and wading through a slough to get to his horses, that were tethered on the bank of a creek, where the grass was growing luxuriantly. She wondered if Mr. Miser was getting any benefit from his revenge. For her part she thought it looked a little serious, when he said he wished there was not a — woman or child in the world. "And it's still raining," exclaimed he.

"We are already as wet as we can be, so what's the difference if it does rain?" remarked Jean.

"Wouldn't we get dry if it stopped raining?" furiously queried Miser with another oath. "If you want anything to drink, just help yourself; there's plenty of water. We can't make coffee."

And they took a chunk of bread, and some dried venison that Allilo had prepared for them, when they were at her camp. She had sent her hunters out, and they had brought in a fine fat deer, the hams of which she had taken and cut into strips, and dried them quickly before the fire, and Jean thought it was the most delicious meat she had ever tasted, as she sat on the horse eating her frugal breakfast.

The baby protested against riding with his father in

the rain, and Jean carried him, though she was chilled and numb and wet. It continued pouring all day long, and all day long they rode, with many a slough to cross, where the horses waded through the water up to their knees. That night they were trying to find a sheltering tree or a rise of ground, but they could find neither. They had taken the west side of the river, and were going down Long Tom. No other alternative remained but to lie down in their wet blankets. It rained for two days. Jean lost all anxiety for herself, and was only thoughtful for her child, who was growing very restless, and showed symptoms of having taken a severe cold. They were still about forty-five miles away from home. Next morning it showed some signs of clearing off. The clouds were shifting, and a strong south wind blowing. The sun shone brightly for one hour. Then the dark clouds began gathering overhead, and it began to pour. They were miles away from any human habitation, and had had no fire for three days by which to warm their freezing limbs, or dry their clothes. Jean's hands were so numb she could scarcely hold the reins. Although she was perched up on the tall horse with a pillow on her lap, the baby resting on the pillow with a blanket about him, her feet often dragged in the water, the sloughs had grown so full and deep. It required some horsemanship to sit there under such conditions. Her horse often plunged into gopher holes, and unless she clung to his back like glue she must topple off. At this juncture, when the water was mid-sides to her horse, Mr. Miser, who had ridden about three rods ahead of her all the journey, making her feel that she had a tender, watchful companion by her side—one that, should an accident befall her, would spring to her aid in a moment, as he did when she had slid down the precipice, and Alillo came to her rescue—he paused a moment, reining up his horse, looked back over his shoulder, and screamed to her that "if she wasn't a cussed fool, and would ride a little faster they might reach the farm-house that stood on the west side of the Willamette river," where Corvallis now stands. Jean said if he would carry the baby, that she would endeavor to keep pace with him. He took the child up like a bag of meal, and tossed him about until he cried so lustily that Jean was compelled to take him. It was now dark. They had ridden up to an empty old cabin, instead of an inhabited farmhouse. Here they found two men who had arrived an hour before them, and were warming themselves at a bright fire. One of the men helped Jean from her horse. Miser took the baby. Jean was so benumbed with the cold she could not stand. The strange men helped her into the house, and set her on a stool in front of the fire. They were not aware of her exhaustion, and she herself was unconscious of it as she fell fainting to the floor. They caught her and laid her on their blankets, already spread for the night, and one of them flew to the river for water which he dashed into her face. When she became conscious, she saw the two men standing by her side, their faces sad with sympathy, and the first sounds that fell upon her ear were the words of Miser assuring the men that she was such a fool that he supposed she fainted at the sight of the fire, not having seen one for so long; that she fainted at a big rock they were coming round, and they were obliged to stay a week at an Indian camp waiting for her recovery. "I'll not stay here a week waiting for her recovery," he told the strangers.

The men inquired how far they had traveled and how far they were to go. Mr. Miser informed them.

CHAPTER XXVIII.

THE DEATH OF JEAN'S BABY.

There was a bright sunshine when they rose next morning. Jean's spirits were greatly revived at the thought of being so near home. And yet it was with the utmost difficulty that she sat on the horse and rode over the road that was comparatively dry land. They had crossed the Willamette River in a ferry-boat, and found the road beaten hard by the heavy rains, so that the horses traveled much faster, and at four o'clock the next day this journey, ever memorable to poor Jean, was ended. Mr. Miser remained a few days. The baby seemed not absolutely ill, and yet not well. Jean and her mother felt alarmed about it, and cautioned Mr. Miser to remain a few days before returning to his ranch. But he said it was only a woman's whim. He could not see but the baby was as well as ever. So without taking the baby in his arms in a last tender embrace, or kissing Jean good-by, he nodded a farewell and rode away.

He had not been gone a week when they buried the baby in the new churchyard. It had gradually grown worse, and being much alarmed, they sent for a physician, who administered a lobelia emetic, which of itself would have killed the child; but the symptoms now being greatly aggravated, they sent for another physician, a young man, very talented, but who at times imbibed too much whisky to command a clear intellect. He gave the baby a whole teaspoonful of calomel. Jean asked if it was calomel, but was assured it was only a harmless chalk. She once reached for the spoon in an agony of despair, knowing that such a dose would kill her child. There was no human pity. This was the most terrible experience of her young life. She must bury her baby! Can you imagine, dear reader, what life seemed to her then, a child in her seventeenth year? She was dazed with grief, stunned with the cold and exposure she had met with. She could not shed a tear. Her heart was like stone when she thought of the ignorant brutality of those doctors that had killed her child, who had been her sole comforter through all those terrible scenes. She was not allowed the poor comfort to sit and moan. They sent for another physician. After hours of excruciating agony, and going down through the valley of the shadow of death, two little infant girls, so helpless they could not cry and so weak they scarcely seemed to breathe, were born and laid in the cradle beside her. Their grandmother said she did not know how, but they went on breathing and living. Afterward, when she could sit up and nurse them tenderly as she could, they could never fill the place of the noble boy that she had laid in the tomb. She could look backward or forward, and life held no bright spot for her. The dreary winter dragged its slow length along. Jean having related some of the horrors of her frontier experience, her mother resolved that when she returned, her brother Will, a boy now sixteen years old, should accompany her back to her home in the mountains.

When the babies were three months old, Mr. Miser came for them in a horse team. This time the parting was wrenching, because the mother and daughter knew they would not meet again for years.

In the fall of '52 a heavy immigration entered the valley, and had scattered themselves pretty thoroughly over it. It was like an oasis in the desert for Jean to meet a human being along this hitherto desolate, unsettled country, and the journey proved to be more enjoyable than any previous one. On their return to the ranch they found that about twenty land claims had been located during the winter by the emigrants of '52, among them one family consisting of man and wife, and a daughter thirteen years of age. Their claim lay just opposite Mr. Miser's. Jean and Mrs. Trent formed a friendship that was close and long-abiding. Jean was now only eighteen, and Hattie Trent fourteen; and they were like two sisters. They could not meet very often, as this dangerous river had to be crossed, and they were a mile and a half apart. On Jean's side of the river there was no family for thirty miles, and many a day she spent alone in her cabin from early morning till dark with no companions but the babies. In the summer, her brother Will arose before daylight, which in Oregon, comes before four o'clock, to drive up the work-cattle. Jean would see him a moment at the breakfast table with the other workmen, then all day long he staid in the mountains splitting rails. Mr. Miser paid his workmen two dollars a day, but made a different bargain with Will Ames, telling him he would pay him one dollar and a half for a hundred rails, put him into a grove where the timber was almost impossible to split, and warned him that if the rails were not of a certain size he would not accept them. Will did not succeed in splitting ten rails a day. When he commenced Jean would often cry over his blistered hands, and make liniment for them. Often the tears of the two children mingled together in sympathy for each other, but Will was the pluckier of the two.

"When I get too disgusted I can get on my horse and ride away, Jean. I would not stay a day only to be with you," he said.

He slept in the barn, after working an hour and a half later than the other men, doing the chores, milking the cows, turning out the oxen, bringing in the wood. All this told on his health. He complained of pain in his lungs, having contracted a severe cold. Jean grew alarmed, and tried to send a letter to her mother through some stranger, who could pass it from one to another, but found no one to undertake the task. She would write one, however, every few weeks, and as no opportunity offered to send it away, she would write another. After months had

THE DEATH OF JEAN'S BABY.

elapsed she succeeded in sending one, and it was full six months before she received an answer. The pony express, that ran from the eastern states to California, had no branch in this country, and the telegraph poles were still growing in the woods.

Miser grew more and more tyrannical and abusive. Having no critical neighbors near by, no check-reins of any kind, he was ruled alone by his masterly qualities of cruelty, miserliness, and treachery. He must buy supplies for the workmen, but he also built a secure outhouse in which to store them, and doled them out as he saw fit. When there were no workmen about, he starved Jean and Will almost to death, and put on his own plate and devoured like a wild animal what he required for his own sustenance, telling Jean that as she was not earning anything, she could live on limited rations. Sometimes his meanness grew so tight that even the workmen were scantily supplied, and Jean's fine cooking, and splendid genius for piecing out a meal, could not overcome it. One day, in the middle of June, when the workmen were much rushed, six stalwart fellows filed into the cabin, and sat down to the table, glistening with polished tin cups, bright as silver, filled with clear, cool fresh water. Two plates filled with snowy white light bread, baked to a delicious brown, were on the table. Jean sat down in her accustomed place with her fresh laundried dress on, her heavy brown hair in smooth coils at the back of her head, gracefully awaiting results. The men took up the cups of water and drank them down in concert. Mr. Miser passed the bread from the head of the table. One or two hungry fellows took a big bite before looking on their plates. The aroma from it was appetizing. A bevy of eyes were leveled upon Jean, expecting her to get up and bring in the dinner from the kitchen, when she simply said: "There is nothing else in the house to cook, and Mr. Miser knew it this morning as well as I." Mr. Miser, in no wise disconcerted, glanced toward Jack Warner, a boyish young fellow, easily imposed upon, and said.

"You go and drive the band of cattle up that are

feeding on the river bottom. There are some fine two-year-old steers." Obeying Mr. Miser's request, they were driven up, one of them shot, and the meat served for a two o'clock dinner. Miser did not swear, as was his custom, at Jean's delaying dinner for ten minutes, as he reckoned this would take sixty minutes off the day's labor, and for punishment he would slide stealthily by Jean, and, unobserved by the workmen, pinch her arm until it was black and blue for days. Tender hearted readers, that have the false idea ingrained into your souls that women mature so much faster than men, if you could have your flesh twisted on your bones as Jean did every day for four years, it might mature your brains, if you are cursed with that commodity, as it resulted in maturing her intellect in time, but not as soon as it would a man's, who had enjoyed this sort of playful domestic felicity.

CHAPTER XXIX.

WHAT IS HONOR?

"It is the hardest luck," remarked Mr. Cursica Miser, with his favorite oath, "that I should be tied to an idiot that is always prating about honor. Now, what is honor? One would think, by the way you talk, it was something to eat, to wear, to hold or handle, or make money with. If you were cold would it warm you? If you were hungry would it feed you? If you had all the honor in the world, do you think people would run to you and pour money into your lap?" This query was rounded by another voluminous oath. "You must have money to live in this world."

"Money can be obtained by honorable means, can it not?" queried Jean with her accustomed far-off look, as she took her baby boy from his rude cot and pressed him closely to her breast with that intensity born of the deep desire of her heart that he might inherit the type of soul that could recognize honor, which she felt the man before her could not do, any more than he could make wings for himself and fly, and the silent cry of her heart went up to the Almighty to save her infant from such deformity of soul—and Jean's mind went wandering off into the boundless fields of metaphysics, trying to feel there was a power in nature that could impart character from the mother and leave the paternal partner ever impotent to harm.

The torture to this child-wife of only twenty was that she could look down into the depths of Cursica Miser's villainies with a magnified keenness of vision, while he could no more comprehend the motives governing her acts in life than a blind man can see the stone that he stumbles over. When they were first married he had tried to conceal his acts from her by keeping silent, but at last, he said, that was useless, for the more secretive he was, the more she read his conduct.

"It would be better if you did not know everything I do," he said, "besides hindering me you are always getting me into scrapes."

"Why, how, what do you mean?" asked Jean, with her great brown eyes gazing wonderingly into his. "What do I do to get you into scrapes, as you call it?"

"Children and fools always tell the truth," responded Mr. Miser.

"Well, does the truth hurt anybody?" innocently inquired Jean.

"Well, don't it?" wrathfully continued Miser, as he swaggered across the puncheon floor with one hand holding his hat a foot above his head, while the other, with the fingers spread wide apart, combed back the offending tuft of hair that always seemed in the way and to require immediate smoothing down, on the top of his head, when his temper was ruffled. His hat being firmly replaced, he seated himself like one resigned to the most galling fate, and summing up his grievance thus, with the most frightfully disgusting sneer on his face, drawled out: "Does the truth hurt anybody? Did it hurt me when you told that it was me that shot into that Indian camp last fall, when the old blind squaws ran out into the hills, too scared to come back, and froze to death before morning? The bucks coming back from their hunt, got up a war that cost the settlement a pile, and the government too. I would have lost my scalp if your innocent truth had reached the Indians two days sooner, before the soldiers captured them. I met some bucks out in the hills and told them it was Bill Trask that shot into their camp, and Bill came within an ace of getting his scalp raised, and now he's mad at me. There were six old blind squaws lying stark, stiff and cold on the side-hill next morning when I rode by. How clear and bright the sun shone out; the weather beamed down as innocently as your truths, on them, all huddled in a heap, just as though it could not be cold and kill. It was a blessing to the camp and to the squaws too, that they were dead and out of their misery. I'll venture that not one of them was less than a hundred and twenty years old, and yet, when the Indian camp got back and found them dead, gods! what a howl they raised! You could hear them ten miles away, up and down this valley, with that infernal chant of theirs. If I live here forever, do you think the neighbors will ever forgive me?"

"No, I guess not, unless that deed is wiped out of their memories by some darker one," Jean answered with a shudder.

"Then you say does the truth hurt anybody?" drawled out Miser, "and yesterday when Kate Mills was here to see Dan Dorrell, you had to up and tell that I was driving one of her father's steers across the river, and I'll bet anything you told her it was the big brown spotted steer with the lopped horn."

"Why, yes, what harm could that do?" with her big brown eyes set wondering again.

"Why, you fool, I beat the steer till its flesh is a mass of steak made tender for the crows. The steer will go straight home and lie down but never get up again. I will have to pay for it, and what will the Mills family think of me? Miss Kate will never visit you again if she *is* dead in love with Dorrell," and Cursica Miser got up and scuffed his heels and strode the floor, continuing:

"When the old Indian chief came and swore vengance and said if I did not take back these boards that I stole off his ancestors' graves to make a floor for your ladyship, that he would hew the whole American nation into little strips and make graves without any covering of boards, you cried and brought him bread, and, by some necromancy, made him think you were a saint and I a bad man."

"There will come a day, maybe," retorted Jean, "when I will not cry so much, but act more."

"It would take one of the best nugget mines ever found in California," Miser went on, not seeming to heed her words, "to improve this ranch as it ought to be. There are miles and miles of fencing to be done, and whenever I get a young fellow to work and can make a good bargain with him, then you take his part and cry and say: 'It's too bad for you not to pay the boys all you owe them; such young fellows out in the world with no mothers to care for them.' There's Bob Jones and Bill Williams that I have paid, and here they come again for pay that I deducted for rainy days and Sundays. Who ever heard of a man's getting wages for work on Sundays or a rainy day? How can a man ever expect to get rich with a woman like you? Those two fellows I got to take up government land for me—of course they spent two years on it, but what's that? they had a good time hunting and fishing; they were good-natured chaps. I did not pay them any money—I gave them those two old Indian ponies, the old flint-lock gun and a pretty good shot-gun. They are not the kind of men whose time is worth anything. They made a big fuss, and got the neighbors to howling about my swindling them out of the land. There was no swindling about it," he continued, pulling his hat down over his eyes, "it was a regular bargain. You thought they ought to be paid, and so I paid each one fifty dollars, and even then the neighbors said I wheedled them out of the land."

"You would not take $5,000 for either of the places now that you have your deed to them," said Jean.

"An old clutchman* told me, confidentially, the other day," said Miser, "that you advised old Chief Nezic, that day he got so mad about my denuding his ancestral tombs,—to kill cattle and get his pay; and to console him

*Meaning "Indian."

still further, you asked him if he did not think the spirits of his departed friends would spurn the boards being brought back and replaced on their graves, after the pale faces had stolen them and walked on them, and all the fine sentiments about desecrating the graves of his beloved dead vanished from the mind of the old savage like the base fabric of a dream as soon as you told him he could exchange the boards for beef. You cautioned him to burn the horns and hoofs to prevent being caught stealing cattle."

"Yes," answered Jean, "I told him all that and more. If I had not, my own life would have been the only one left to tell how the war began. That tuft of hair that you comb up with your fingers so much would have been dangling at the belt of the old chief long ago, along with the scalps of all the other whites along the river." And Mr. Miser, with more serious candor on his countenance than it usually wore, taunted her with "You would have been spared, no doubt. You have a charmed life that the Indians all respect."

"Not that at all," answered Jean, "but my first act after landing here was to dress the poor little idiot boy's feet, who had kicked over a pot of boiling water on them while asleep, scalding the flesh horribly. I washed them and dressed them with clean cloths every day until Alillo came, from her trip in the mountains after berries, and she took the task off my hands."

"And he's your servant to-day?"

"Yes, my faithful, willing servant, and rather a bright boy, too, considering the Indians called him a 'pilton'* before I took him in hand."

"And so you confess you told the old buck to kill cattle?"

"Yes. Why not be honorable with the Indians? Had I not come into their country, bringing droves of cattle, thousands of head, to feed on their grass? Do not I eat their deer, killed by the whites? If we kill their deer, why should they not kill our cattle? Can

* Pilton, meaning fool.

we, the superior race, come in here, taking their land, game, fish, berries, everything, and ask them to stand still and starve to death? I cannot and will not do it. There is no honor nor justice in it."

"There you go again—honor!"

"Yes, honor. The wildest Indian I ever met will not let me do him a kindness without almost immediately returning it fourfold. If I tell one to sit by my fire to warm on a cold day, or give him a good dinner, as I do lots of times, or even a piece of bread, he will come soon with a great fat venison ham, or a basket of delicious wild berries, nestling in forest leaves, to cater to my delicate taste; or perhaps a string of those glorious mountain trout, or a buckskin, beautiful and soft as velvet, all of which put my little acts to shame. And Alillo has brought me so many new baskets, that are so useful I could not keep house without them. What would life be without my otter, beaver, bear, wolf, and skunk skins to cover this old puncheon floor? I tell you, the Indian character in its native wildness is grand, until stung to revenge by the villainies of the whites."

"And Alillo is your *sister*."

"Yes, my sweet, wildwood sister, that I can trust my babies with."

"Oh, *you* can trust any Indian."

"That is so; I have not met with one act of treachery yet from an Indian. I cannot conjure up a shadow of fear, now that I have lived with them so long; that is, a near neighbor, with very amicable and friendly relations. I, a marauder and foreigner in their country! If a war should break out to-day I should be safe from the savages' tomahawk."

"Because you feed them on beef?" queried Miser, with one of his most quizzical smiles.

"Yes, because I try to act honorably with them, and they know it."

"Still prating about honor. I should like to know what it is. It's some d—— necromancy that's past

"Oh, oh, Mimiloose, Mimiloose."

my comprehension. It is a very convenient, adaptable kind of arrangement. Everything I do by the Indians is thieving, and everything you do is honorable. When I found where the Indians had 'cached' their winter's wheat, on the banks of the river, in the dry land, intending to have a good time eating 'sapalilli' when they returned from their hunt, I took Mike Riley, the wagon, old Towser and the shot-gun, and raised their 'cache' and hauled it into camp and stored it in my granary—fifty bushels of the finest white wheat I ever saw. Those old squaws had winnowed out every bit of dust and chaff. There wasn't a shriveled-up kernel of wheat in the whole lot."

"And you can't see that it was a mean act? You hired those old squaws to work in the harvest field and you didn't pay them a cent, only allowing them to glean the scattered heads of wheat in the stubble fields, and when they had picked up the heads one by one and thrashed them in their baskets, and winnowed them by blowing out the chaff and dust, then you went in the night in their absence and hauled it in and locked it up in your granary, and don't know it's an act that ought to bring on a war of extermination—of at least yourself."

Jean had scarcely uttered these words, when Allilo came flying into her cabin, her long hair unbraided and flying, her whole dress in the wildest confusion. She flung herself on the floor and rocked herself to and fro, and as soon as she could speak said, in her own language:

"The Rogue Rivers are fighting on Cow Creek, and my father and twenty braves have gone to join them— Oh, oh, Mimiloose, Mimiloose!" (meaning, they will be killed.) In an instant, old Chief Nezic came rushing in, and with excited gestures and wild pantomime, showed how the battle was on—the Indians shooting, and pale faces falling everywhere, their houses burned, their cattle killed for vengeance.

In a moment more, two horsemen galloped up at full

speed, and confirmed the news that was too true. The whole country was in arms. The next day it was learned that eight or ten families along the road had been taken by surprise, all murdered, and their cabins burned; but the settlers, volunteer soldiers, flew to arms, and drove the savages back to their stronghold in the mountains.

The war lasted two years. But the Indians were held in check first by the volunteer soldiers and then by the regular troops. At last a treaty of peace was made and the Indians taken to their reservations, and a pretension by the government to pay the Indians for this land, and another pretension to pay the settlers for their lost property and time and money spent in the Indian wars.

CHAPTER XXX.

A NIGHT OF HORROR.

The bravery of a woman, a Mrs. Harris, really held the Indians at bay and checked the massacre on that terrible night, June —, '54. Her husband, standing in the doorway of their cabin at dusk, was shot. His undaunted wife dragged his mutilated and dying body into the house, while the bullets from the savages whistled by her head. As quick as thought she shut and fastened the door, and learning from the lips of her dying husband how to load and fire the rifle, she defended her little castle like a heroine. A bullet from an Indian hit her little boy, a lad of twelve, in the arm, and before the echo from his gun had died away, she sprang to the window and taking an unerring aim, poured the contents of her rifle into the Indian's body, who with a yell fell dead to the ground. The Indians then fell back to some bushes near by, where they kept up a deadly fire through the window at any object that might be seen moving in the house. For twelve hours this brave woman stood there with her tried and trusty rifle, loading and firing, while her dead husband lay at her feet, her only child, wounded and pale as the clay-cold corpse of his father, molding the bullets. All that fearful night the savages rent the air with their war-whoops, and danced around with their threatening torches. The day at length broke and found her ammunition well-nigh spent, with no hope of assistance, and the awful fate staring her in the face of being burnt alive, with her boy, in her house, when lo! upon the hills she heard the tramp of horses and beheld a troop of mounted men dashing towards her house. On, on they came like the wind, finding for miles and miles on their route waste, desolation, smouldering ruins and charred and mutilated bodies, till here, at daybreak, they found this heroic woman and brave boy and rescued them from the torch, bullet, bayonet and scalping-knife of those murderous savages.

And though these things were going on all around her, yet Jean feared not for the safety of herself and babes.

Indians have a quick perception; they knew she was their friend and they pitied her. She felt they would not murder her. The settlers in her neighborhood said she was foolhardy, because she chose to stay in her cabin rather than go into the block-house, and endure the hardships and dangers of a frontier fort life. The secret was, she had to stay. Mr. Miser actually refused to take her and her three little babies to the fort, but left her all the days alone, while he hid in the bushes for safety, and when the night came on, this gallant, pale-faced chieftain, this brave husband and father, would leave them in the house while he crawled into a hollow log or under the hay-mow, so as to be free, in case of an attack, to make his escape.

There was not a family left in all that broad country but was compelled to go into forts for protection, excepting Jean and her babes. And she, with the protection of one negro servant, a watch-dog, and half a dozen guns, remained alone in her cabin day and night, through all the horror of this Indian war.

During the Rogue River war the citizens between North and South Umpqua were forted-up from ten days to six weeks; the braver ones getting out and risking their lives to defend their homes and their property. The more timid ones remained in the fort, which was built by digging trenches around a half acre of ground. Trees, a foot in diameter, were chopped and set down in the trenches to form a wall twenty feet high. For greater security, inside the wall, huts made of split logs were built.

We will leave it to the imagination of the reader what the horror of this forting-up meant to the pioneer settlers.

A NIGHT OF HORROR.

From a hundred to a hundred and fifty people found security within those walls.

It was exceedingly provoking and somewhat ludicrous to the average citizen on the North Umpqua to discover, after enduring the horror of the fort life, that the Indians were more afraid of the whites than the whites were of the Indians, who fled to the mountain fastnesses where they had plenty of room, bright, sparkling waterfalls, splendid trout and the grandest scenery in the world. They feasted on elk, bear, deer and berries, returning to the valley fat and sleek, with loads of supplies for the winter.

Weeks passed without any communication between the whites and this North Umpqua tribe of Indians.

A rumor had gone forth that this tribe had gone to the head waters of the Umpqua, to be reinforced by the Shastas, a very numerous and warlike tribe of Indians that never condescended to come down to the valley. They were large, stalwart men, of much greater intelligence than the average Indian, and were a race of undaunted courage and bravery, and greatly to be feared.

The volunteer soldiers becoming restless, our deliberate government having at length sent instructions to them to make a treaty of peace, they sent scouts in every direction to try to communicate with the Indians, but it was useless. The soldiers had been camped for six days on Mr. Miser's broad pastures. The horses were foraging off two well-stored barns. One fat steer after another had been slaughtered; the stores of vegetables were being hopelessly reduced, and Miser said he thought Jean was quite as well protected as though she had gone to the fort, and if he had known the United States troops were to entertain such friendly and protecting relations to him, he would have preferred being forted. Miser held a long confidential talk with the captain, and told him he would like to have "this farce end." The captain informed Jean that Miser had just given him some very important news—that the Indians had so much confidence in her that they would believe every word she said.

"Yes, but how can my voice reach them," answered Jean. "It is not so stentorian that it can be heard twenty miles away."

"There was a camp-fire found this morning where two Indians and a squaw must have slept last night, about ten miles away, so if you will consent to ride at the head of our column this morning, we will try, with your presence and a white flag, to gain their attention. These must be Indian spies sent back to reconnoitre, and no doubt intend, from Mr. Miser's remarks, to confer with you."

In an hour, Jean was on her saddle-horse and in company with the captain and two lieutenants, was galloping in the direction of the camp-fire. They were clambering over a frightful gorge through a narrow footpath, when a ball of twisted grass and dried leaves was tossed into Jean's lap. It seemed to fall straight from the sky, but on the steep mountain side above, they saw the bushes moving, and Jean's clear voice floated out in the morning air, "Alillo!" and the silvery, liquid tones came ringing down the mountain side "Tillicum, tillicum!" (meaning friend). And the war was ended and peace commenced in the mingling of these voices. After holding a long conference with the Indians, Jean went back home proud, triumphant, and happy, with Alillo as a prisoner of war.

Within two days, every Indian on the river was brought in, and camped at the head of the valley, but they utterly refused to hold a treaty with the soldiers, and again the captain was puzzled, and held a "powwow" with Miser, and soon an invitation was sent to Jean and Alillo to join them, and at last it was decided that if Jean would go to the camp, and make a speech to the Indians, telling them that the government would do thus and so, they would listen. Accordingly, next morning, Jean, with the captain, at the head of the column of soldiers, confronted an army of braves who stood with their arms folded on their breasts, without

Jean's deep sympathy for them moved her to tears, and she knelt under the white flag.

moving a muscle or giving a grunt of recognition, as stolid as iron posts. Jean's deep sympathy for them moved her to tears, and she knelt under the white flag, the cool morning air fanning the brows of that column of stalwart red men, facing their pale-faced brothers, listening to the words of the one white person of the white race, who would, they believed, speak the truth. But her prayer to Almighty God, pronounced in their presence, proved how utterly void of truth she believed her words to be.

"Oh, Almighty God, Father alike of the red and the white man, thou hast the power to compel the men of our mighty nation to keep the treaty now about to be signed between these two nations of red and white men. Grant, oh, God, that my words may be kept—in letter and in deed, truthfully kept." And a clear, distinct "Amen!" as of one voice, was pronounced by the column of men. The Indians bowed their heads.

Jean, rising, went on with her speech. She told the Indians that the government had promised to buy their land, paying them so much annuity. But the Indians were to leave their homes, and go to Grand Round Valley, in Yam Hill county, where there was already a reservation.

The treaty was signed by all except old Chief Nezic, who buried his face in the sand, telling the young men that they could sign it, but he could not sell the graves of his fathers for money, nor blankets, nor horses, nor food; he wanted to be buried there with his fathers. The young bucks said they had no notion of being buried; that the whites traveled, and they could.

The government then sent teams, and removed the Indians, with all their household accouterments, to the reservation—dogs, ponies, guns, everything—one hundred and fifty miles away. When they started, they made the valleys ring with the same funeral chant that they make over the dead. It was something terrific, that last howl that the Indians ever made in that Umpqua Valley. It rang out in the crisp morning air, that sad November day. The march was terrible to them, leaving the homes that had been theirs through all time that their stories or memories could retain. Another, stronger — a white — race had dispossessed them.

Jean's brothers, Will Ames and Dan Murdstone, were in the Cayoose and Bannock Indian wars, fighting every year, from the first settlement of the country until peace reigned in every hamlet, hill-top, valley and village, from end to end of the Pacific Coast—faithful, valiant, volunteers, soldiers, cavalrymen riding their own horses, wearing clothing earned by the hard toil of frontier life, buying their own supplies, using their own guns, and supplying their own ammunition. And our much-loved Uncle Sam is to-day in the peaceful possession of all this vast domain, wrested by the bravery of her brothers and other early pioneers who risked their lives and fortunes, and to-day lie in peaceful, unmarked, unhonored graves, dying in the prime of their early manhood while protecting the frontier settlements from the Indians. Has the government ever paid one dollar of its debt? We hope some day it may, for the memory of those brave boys who kept their war-scrip so sacredly. It was high treason, in their opinion, to think that the government would not faithfully pay its Indian war debts.

Jean heard this reiterated a thousand times, and her blood boiled with the memory that her brothers were lying in their peaceful graves, having spent their lives in the sacred cause of peace and the security of their homes; and dying, God intrusted their orphan children to Jean to rear and educate.

The government cannot lay claim to any territory over which war was ever waged under the broad canopy of heaven, that is equal in value to the Pacific Coast, and this being true, so honorable a debt should have been liquidated long ago by our honorable government. This is history.

The volunteer soldiers should be paid for their time,

for the defense of their homes, and for the wresting of these vast landed estates from their original owners, the Indians, and securing them peaceably to the government.

CHAPTER XXXI.

"I WILL STILL BE MYSELF."

Now that the Indians had gone, Mr. Cursica Miser immediately gave his whole war ability to his family—not that he had ever at any time distinguished himself in any open warfare with the Indians; but Jean soon discovered that the presence of the Indians had been a great check to Mr. Miser's indulging his propensity to cruelty to his family. His cruelties and constant ill-usage at length resulted in an overwhelming disaster, not to the family peace, for it never had any, but to the family union.

The Indian boy servant, Caweecha, who would not consent to leave his mistress, when the Indians went to the reservation, was out milking the cows. The family were seated at the breakfast table, which was set in the middle of the cabin floor, that was ornamented with a variety of handsome skins. A bank of wild roses, fragrant and blooming, with hanging vines, wild grasses, and pine cones, stood at the left on a rude bench. A small mirror ornamented the mantel, beneath which burned a cheerful fire in the wide-mouthed fire-place. A few draperies hung here and there about the room, and a rude book-shelf that Jean herself had constructed contained a few well-thumbed books of standard authors, most of which were borrowed from a neighboring library—Mr. Dan. Stewart's. The little twin girls sat opposite Jean and her baby boy. Mr. Miser, at the head of the table, was swallowing his breakfast like a ravenous wolf, when his son and heir to his vast estates espied the breakfast disappearing so rapidly, and not being old enough to express himself, made desperate efforts to make himself understood by violent kicks and gestures, signifying that he wanted an equal amount of food, whereupon Jean gave him an egg. But he wanted more, and she gave him another. It was clear that the ambition of the young man knew no bounds. He wanted everything on the table put on his plate. His mother, Jean, was trying with firm though gentle tones to quell the disturbance.

Mr. Miser arose unceremoniously, put on his hat, and left the room. Jean supposed he had gone to his business. The baby boy was now quietly finishing his breakfast. Mr. Miser returned looking like a demon, with a tough, thrifty hazel three-quarters of an inch thick and five feet long. He walked hastily to the baby, snatching him from his chair and holding him by one arm a foot or two from the floor, and after a few withes on the back of the baby, Jean, not being able to stop him, and knowing the child would die in Miser's hands, she bent over it to protect it from the blows, and the fierce strokes that fell on her neck and shoulders made her thankful in her heart that she could shield her child from such agony. Each blow from the infuriated monster was like a knife thrust. When the stick had been beaten to splinters, he stopped and not till then; and when Jean could recover her breath to speak, she said: "Your blows have divorced us!" And no truer words did her lips ever utter.

For awhile she forgot her own misery in her pity for her child writhing in pain. Miser left the house, and Jean had no time for tears that day. She had suffering to relieve that is not often witnessed. She did not realize the severity of her own wounds until she had tried to lie down at night, and found it impossible. The child's life was despaired of for days.

Caweecha came in with the pails brimful of milk, and glancing at the baby who was writhing in excruciating pain, sprang quickly to Jean's side, asking in deepest tones of alarm and sympathy: "Burned?"

"Gods, yes, Caweecha, burned!" she answered.

Miser had thrown the club into the fire and jumped on his horse and rode away. He told Caweecha he was going to Roseburg, and Jean very indiscreetly said, "I wish he would never return."

In an instant Caweecha, with the quick perception an Indian, said, "Miser did it. Me kill him! **Me heap kill!**"

Jean's **soul was** wild with passion, and while she would have been glad to **see** the man dead, yet she was horrified at the thought of stirring her faithful servant **to kill him.** While smarting under his stinging lash, **she could lie to screen** his life. She knew if her servant got an inkling of the blood trickling through her dress that nothing would save Miser's life from his revenge. Caweecha brought her water and asked to go for her neighbor, Mrs. Trent.

No; no neighbor to see her bleeding back! She could not bear that humility. And Caweecha again looking searchingly into her **eyes,** said:

"Miser did it. Me know. He heap look mesacha.* Me cumtux."†

This **was in '56. The blood of the** nation **was not** yet flowing **to free negro slaves.**

Under some pretense the faithful Caweecha must be sent away while Jean could dress the wounds of herself **and** child. She told him to go and saddle his horse, as **she** might need to send him for the doctor. Indeed, it seemed quite probable. She then cut the child's clothes from his arms, and hastily dressed his wounds. She as quickly tore off her own blood-stained clothes and hid them away, as though she were the murderer and had done this brutal deed. Her pride was working her a great wrong by covering up the crime, but she was a child and did not know it. Besides, she thought the taunts and jeers of the world would be more than her lacerated flesh and wounded heart could endure. She could bear **this** quietly, and she would. She was the metal they make heroines of. She said St. Paul had endured **stripes** without a murmur, and she could.

She **told** Miser, on **his** return, to occupy another

*Mesacha, meaning "bad." †Cumtux, "to understand."

room, away from her and the children, which he did without one word ever passing between them on the subject. They were divorced. She still lived under the same roof, but found life much more endurable since the beating than it had ever been while she was the monster's wife.

She remained in the cabin a year and a half in daily fear of her life, thanking God for the privilege of caring for her children. She trembled as one standing over an earthquake, knowing full well there must come an end to her present life. Miser rarely spoke to her, or took any notice of the children. She was only too content to be spared the attention of the brute.

Jean did not let her lips pronounce a word of his unkindness to her. She knew how, like a blighting mildew, it had withered every bright hope of her young, buoyant heart. And how could her mother, who had passed through so many bitter trials, bear to know that she was not happy. No! she would let this aching grief, like corroding rust, eat out her heart's core before she would add another woe to those already there, and with more bravery than it ever took to face a cannon-ball, she said mentally, "I *will* be brave and stand face to face with stubborn fate." She made a desperate struggle to conceal her real feelings from every one, and tried hard to do each task assigned her as cheerfully as possible. Jean had friends, with hearts deep and true as ever throbbed in human breast, and though her lips spoke never a syllable of his cruelties to her, yet every one knew she was a slave.

Though she tried hard to conceal her real life, and to be to the world a living lie, yet she could not; for looks speak the truth louder than tongues ever do. And when in 1857, she rose in her puny might and vowed she would be free, and be no longer Miser's legalized slave, do you think she had not counted the cost?—ay, the cost of having her innocent babes torn from her crushed and bleeding heart and given into the custody of the monster who had nearly killed her

13

and her child? Strong men, gray-haired men, came to her convulsed with grief, tears falling like rain, warning her against such a step, saying the law would show her no mercy, that her children would be taken from her, her character destroyed, and she, with a broken heart, blighted health, and defamed reputation, turned out into the cold charities of a selfish world to die, or perhaps end her days in a house of prostitution. She *thanked* them for that last word, and said:

"I end *my* days in such a place! God never made me to fill such a position. All the laws and law-makers on earth can't ruin *me*. I will still be myself."

"Yes, but your husband has all the money, and he will use it against you," they said.

"He will not try to injure the character of the mother of his innocent babes, will he?"

"Yes, he will, and mark the words, he will succeed."

"And this is the fiend you would have me live with, and bear children for a life-time."

"Yes, 'tis better than to try to escape. Society will thrust you out; you will be a doomed woman; your life won't be long, and 'tis better to bear it all quietly and sink into an early grave; there you will find peace."

"I do not fear to die," she said. "I have longed for death, but now I will live; the world needs me. I will first free myself, then I will espouse the cause of my oppressed sisters. I will be an abolitionist, and work for the abolition of white woman slavery. I should despise myself if I should sit down here to die, a stupid slave, an ignominious death. No, I will live, and *you mark my words*, if the laws of my country treat me as you say they will, I will bear it; but *the world shall know it!* If I am to be a martyr, I will be a heroine also. What! shall I live on the life I've been living, continue to wear out my life in bondage, and leave the same fate to my daughters?"

CHAPTER XXXII.

A VISITOR.

Jean had scarcely recovered from the effects of the conflict with Miser, when one day, Mr. Dan Stewart called, accompanied by a friend, a gentleman of leisure, who had come to while away the summer months with him at his camp, ten miles away, on the river. Mrs. Stewart would join them in a month, when the pleasure party would be complete. Mrs. Stewart's niece and an unmarried sister would accompany her, riding, boating, fishing, and the general fun of summer camp-life in the mountains, to be enjoyed by the party. Mr. Stewart was a gentleman of rare ability. He enjoyed a good book as he did a fine landscape. Sitting in his tent door, like Jacob of old, with his cattle on a thousand hills, the sun's low beams gilding hill-top and mountain with radiant splendor; the dark waters of the North Umpqua rolling over its rocky bed, or winding in and out of some steep wall that pent it in so narrow a channel that it looked like a silvery thread, wound in and out from valley, hill and mountain; for within the scope of the eye, there was diversified country with beauty and grandeur rarely to be met with even in nature's grand panorama, whose wealth of wondrous beauty had been flung with the prodigal hand of the Almighty—Stewart would almost shed tears, in his rapture over this landscape, that he had not studied painting in his younger days, so that he might catch the marvelous beauty on canvas; but alas, for the golden opportunities squandered in youth! The gentleman who called with Mr. Stewart was of medium stature, light brown hair, deep blue eyes, a Grecian nose, broad chin, full round lips, chiseled to perfection. You knew the moment you **saw the man that** candor, purity of **sentiment,** and honest purpose, **were the** ruling powers **of his mind.** Mr. Stewart's leading in the brilliant **conversation that** he and Jean indulged in, **for** the **next half hour, gave** his friend, **a man of** more depth **and** reserve **force,** little opportunity **for** showing Jean what kind of man he was. But **for all** that, from the first moment their eyes met, a subtle power had taken possession of her; she longed to know the man, as she had never longed **to** know a human being before in her life. She felt if she could know that man, she could tell him her hidden griefs. She was sure the tear-stain on her face, hidden by smiles **and** gay **words** from Mr. Stewart, were observed by the stranger.

An hour after, when they rose to go, it was like parting with a friend she had known and loved, **and** she would never see him again! Was fate **so cruel?** As they were about to go, the stranger pulled **a novel** from his coat-pocket, saying:

"Your friend, Mr. Stewart, would like to read **this** book, perhaps?"—**adding to Jean:** "We have just finished it; **we shall enjoy talking it over** when **we meet** again."

It was "The Tower of London," by Dumas.

Her heart gave a great bound for joy—that he wished **to see her** again. This was rapture. Jean, wholly unaccustomed to joy of any kind, was about to despair of the world holding that commodity for her. As the **man** held out the book, a thrill of pain, joy, pleasure— what was it?—pervaded her whole being. It was bliss to her to know there was love in the world. She took the book; her eyes met the stranger's; the gentlemen bowed, were **on** their horses, and gone in a moment.

She stood holding the book, riveted to the spot. **It** was transformed to the holy of all holies, the **place** she had met the stranger. How long she stood, transfigured, glorified **by** God's law of holy **love,** she never knew. From **that time she** was a woman, thrilled with the power of **love.** She thought of nothing for

Her heart gave a great bound for joy.

days, only that she was in ecstasy, that she existed. Some day she might be a widow; then if she should meet the handsome stranger, who called that day, the horror of all she had passed through would only enhance her pleasure when she had some one to love, to speak words of sympathy and tenderness to her.

Love! oh, life! oh bliss! Would such a day ever come, hemmed in with every obstacle to such a possible ending. Then her thoughts would turn back to the dull, sober truth, the hateful reality, and sighing, she would say to herself; "Bright thoughts are better for me, and as God has given them me and a brain to think with that nobody can control, I will do as I please with my thoughts. If 'tis wicked to wish to be happy, then I am going to be wicked. I am going to think of love and what the bliss might be if I had a husband to love me. If when a girl at my mother's the stranger had called, what would life have been, when only to think of it now is such joy." How glorious to be relieved of the companionship of Mr. Miser. He no longer takes the trouble to inform her, every few days, that she has not as much sense as a "yaller dog," no longer tells her he will tie a stone about her neck and drown her in the river, no longer slides stealthily by her side and familiarly pinches the flesh on her arm till 'tis black as a coal for days. All these little attentions are dispensed with, to her great joy. A dignified silence reigns between them, except when someone is by, and then, only to ward off suspicion, a few words pass between them. She is in delight to be a child with her children. She weaves fancies that she and they will grow up together, possibly go to school together. She will be as good as gold looking after every interest on the great ranch; money is pouring in, like golden streams. They must be immensely wealthy if this continues, and in time she will be a woman, with a woman's sense. She has read somewhere that intellect rules, and she is beginning to find that she has rather a bright mind. And if all this be true, she says, "There must be hope ahead for me."

One day, however, **Miser** asked **her** to go boat-riding. She looked up in astonishment. His eyes fell, showing plainly some evil intention, and he walked quickly away as if he had suddenly changed his mind. They did not go that day. Jean thought nothing of this the first day, and would have gone had **he** persisted. The next day, **when he** asked **again,** she declined with some trivial excuse, but her suspicions were aroused. When he came the third day with the old-time sinister smile, she refused. He insisted, and was about to use force to take **her into the boat,** together with the three children. Her **loud screams** brought a man who was chopping timber **across the river,** to her assistance, and the would-be murderer slunk away.

Jean now knew it was impossible for her to remain there any longer. She took her babe in her **arms,** and moving toward the glass to **see** if her **countenance** betrayed the terrible agony of **soul** that stirred within **her** at the thought **of being separated an hour from** her darling children; **her attention was** drawn toward her sweet little five-**year-old Ella,** almost her second self, who, fearful **of some impending** crisis, had climbed upon a **stool near the glass,** and seemed the picture of despair, **as she said in accents** of the deepest sadness, "O, mother, take me, too!" Jean saw only her face, **and could** never forget her looks. It seemed to Jean **her** words would kill her. Her looks, so deep, so full **of** terrible meaning, as though she "knew it all;" the tone so tenderly beseeching, "O, mother, take me, too!" The sound died away with the moment, but the impression in her heart could never die. Had she wavered now in her resolution and stayed a few days longer, she must have **sunk** down to **a** watery grave. She was convinced now **that** Miser's thought, given at first only **as a** threat to **make her** fear him, had crystalized into **a determination to act upon it,** and not only tie a stone **about her neck, but to drown** her children with her, as he had threatened to do **a** thousand times during the **four** years they had lived on the banks of **the** dark, flowing waters of the Umpqua river. But she must live—

live for her children. Life seemed worth all it would cost her. In the family of a friend she found shelter for a short time, until Thomas Ames came to take her and her children to her mother's.

Miser compelled Jean to see a lawyer with him about getting a divorce before he would allow her to take the children and go to her mother's. So they went.

CHAPTER XXXIII.

LAWYER GOBBS.

The lawyer's office was in the back room of an old wooden building used as a hotel. The great man, lawyer Gobbs of Roseburg, since governor of Oregon, sat with his legs crossed, as if to assist in holding up the ponderous proportions above. He had a large frame, but it looked diminutive when compared with his mammoth stomach, which seemed to swell out like a gigantic protuberance on the side of a gnarled oak-tree. His eyebrows were dense, coarse, brown and shaggy, and he looked to Jean as though he might have been at least half brother to the grizzly bear that roams the Sierras and had just gorged himself on an unprotected ranch of Digger Indian children. He seemed to understand their errand, and addressing his conversation to Miser, at length asked, "What is the trouble between you?" Miser replied, "Ask her, she is the one; I am not dissatisfied, she is the one." The lawyer took no notice of Jean. She didn't carry the purse. But annoyed at Miser's answer, and knitting his shaggy brow, queried again, "Is there not some cause for jealousy? I see there is a great disparity in your years." Miser, not understanding how necessary a plea of adultery is in an action for a successful divorce, for once told the truth, and growing incoherent, he swore there was no cause for jealousy, and the man that would accuse him of such a thing was a liar. At this, the lawyer grew more perplexed, and taking rapid strides across the room, that shook the whole house, while a new thought lighted up his dull, phlegmatic face, he said, motioning his finger to Miser, "Come with me;" and they withdrew to another apartment for a private interview. In a few minutes they returned. Jean left the office, and Miser followed her, saying he wanted to talk with her a little privately, and proceeding, he said: "The lawyer tells me that neither of us can get a divorce unless I can prove that you have been false to your marriage vows." With the blood standing still in her veins, Jean replied, "You can never do that."

"I know it, and I told the lawyer so, that you are as pure as an angel, and that your name is untarnished. 'I will arrange that matter,' the lawyer said. 'If we can't prove any actual guilt, 'tis easy to hunt up slanderous stories to blacken women's characters; we always do in such cases; 'tis nothing. You get some of your hired men, or your neighbors, anybody, to start the reports, and I will see that they are circulated. I keep a hotel, and I will make them the table-talk among my boarders. You know how ready men are to believe anything that is said against the character of any woman. If we can make it appear that your wife has been in the least indiscreet, we'll have no trouble in getting you a divorce, and giving the children to you. This is the cheapest. 'Twill save all your money for you, and in fact is the only practical course to pursue.'

This was the plot of the lawyer, as near as Miser could tell it, and then he said to Jean, placing his thumb firmly over his finger: "I've got you right under my thumb, and I will do with you as I please, unless you drop this thing, and go home and live with me as my wife."

No language can express the utter contempt she felt for him then. If she hated him before, she despised herself for ever having seen such an unprincipled wretch, and with indignation flashing in her eyes, she said, "You can't do so damning a deed, and if there are such foul fiends on earth I want to know it." To live with such an inhuman monster would be like throwing innocent babes into the jaws of a crocodile to appease his wrath. Her first impulse was to fly from his presence. Then came those piteous, beseeching tones—"O, mother, take me, too!" and the little arms, "all white and dimpled," stretched out so imploringly to her for help—and she thought of the terrible desolation of their lives without a mother's care. They might be fed and clothed by other hands. But oh, who could supply them with their God-given heritage—a mother's love? "It is not all of life to live."

It was in that hour that she found she could talk; and there, on her horse, she plead with him, the father of her children; earnestly and well she told him that the lawyer was a demon in human form, and if he gave heed to such plottings, he, and not she, would be the ruined one, that he would take his money and give him nothing for it.

"Any man that will talk," said Jean, "as you say that lawyer did to you, will do anything for money. I wonder that you can trust him."

Then Jean tried to make him understand how eager and hungry the poor fellow Gobbs was for the case; that he cared for nothing but his gold. She knew she could touch his heart only through his pocket; so she showed him how much less expense 'twould be for her to take the children to her mother's than for him to have them taken care of. He consented, and she took her children and came out of the wilderness a hundred and fifty miles to her mother's. But the little leaven started there in that law office had leavened the whole lump. From that bear's den, in every direction, the very air was filled with the vilest, blackest tales of slander, which had even reached her poor old mother before her. It was midnight when she reached home. Her mother came out to meet her in her night-clothes. For a moment she held her at arm's length, as if by her searching glances, even in the moonbeams' pale light, she would read the secrets of her soul. The *doomed woman* that her gray-haired friends had warned her that she would become, flashed through her mind as a sickening certainty, as she said: "Oh God! mother,

I am as pure as when you received me from His hands," And they both fell to the ground and thanked God that it was so.

Jean was now safe at home in the society of her family, with her precious children by her side. They were doubly dear to her now, as every day the horror was hanging over her that they might be taken from her. At last, her worst fears were realized, as Miser soon came, like a heathen monster, and tore her little children from the arms of their wretched mother, in spite of their piteous cries to stay, and dragged them back to his home in the mountains. He wrote to the Atlantic States in succession for his mother, aunt, cousins, sister, and niece, who, each in turn, tried to live with him, but soon found they could not, and left him alone in his meanness. He then sent for a discarded brother-in-law, who was already in a decline, and needed constant care himself. There, in that old log-cabin, without one comfort in life, with none but this feeble old man to care for them, did the court decide that the children should stay, and after that old man, just tottering on the brink of the grave, had sworn falsely in court, had acted as agent in distributing bribes among other hired witnesses, and done the house work for Miser and his children, deeded his three hundred and twenty acre land claim, and given him all his personal property; yet, when he was of no further service to him, he was driven out, notwithstanding he had a writtten agreement for shelter, care and nursing in Miser's house, for his few declining years.

The poor old victim begged his way to Mrs. Murdstone, saying he could not die in peace until he had sworn to a confession of what he and others had done to effect her daughter's ruin. Mrs. Murdstone took him in, and cared for him in his last hours, like a sister. He died, and the Odd Fellows gave his body a brotherly burial, but the affidavit from his dying lips, sworn to before a justice of the peace, still lives.

After her children were torn from her and taken

back to the hut, Jean soon followed, and when their father told her that his lawyer had advised him not to allow her to see them, Jean could not believe such baseness could find a place in a human breast; but the next day she was forced to, when this shaggy-browed monster, the lawyer himself, rushed into the room where she was locked in the embrace of her children, having just clasped them to her bosom for the first time in four months, and dragged them screaming from the room, and hurried them away, she knew not where.

This lawyer was the same man who, years after, was Governor of Oregon, and later, was candidate for the United States Senate on the Republican ticket, and lost by only one vote. The man who would have cast the one vote required was missing from the legislative hall at the time the final vote was taken. The speaker of the Senate brought down his gavel with great force, but to no purpose, as he sent the sergeant-at-arms to find the missing man. Now, it happened that Thomas Ames, as Dr. Knight had predicted years and years before, was a stalwart among his confreres in the legislative hall that session. He forced measures, and said to Jean:

"I'll die on that floor, Sis, before a man vile as I know that lawyer to be, shall represent Oregon in the Senate of the United States. Never, while I'm alive, shall that man go."

And when the gentleman could not be found, Thomas Ames was the only man on the floor who could guess where he was, and *he* did not know his exact location.

Thomas Ames, who had driven furiously into town, and was the first man in the Senate-chamber that afternoon, leaning toward his confrere in the next seat, quietly, though with something of tragedy in his manner, exclaimed: "I have him now upon the hip, and I'll feed fat upon the ancient grudge I bear him."

It is more than likely that there were more tears shed

and taller oaths indulged in, at the disappointment of this candidate, than any other since Oregon has been a state.

Baby Murdstone was now a girl of nineteen, a strong, resolute, handsome girl. The man who was missing when so much needed, had often, of late, been invited by Thomas Ames to dine with him at the Murdstone farm-house, six miles in the country. Miss Murdstone was charming—in fact, she was fascinating to the gentleman who was so stanch a political friend of the aspirant for senatorial honors.

On the day that the final vote was to be cast, Thomas Ames met the friend, and taking out his watch, said:

"My friend, it is eleven o'clock. We've just time to drive to the Murdstones' and lunch on fried chicken with peaches and cream."

"Only too happy to join you," said the fly.

Miss Murdstone met them at the gate and assured them that dinner had been waiting five minutes. The gentleman thought he never had seen Miss Murdstone more charming than to-day. Dinner was soon dispatched, Thomas declaring that the affairs of state were hanging heavy upon their massive brows that day.

"I don't like statesmen, I like gentlemen of leisure," poutingly rejoined Miss Murdstone, adding with most bewitching grace that she wanted to drive to town with her brother to buy a ribbon for her new hat.

The noble politician deplored her entertaining such an opinion, and assured her if she would consent to ride with him that the affairs of state should not prevent her from obtaining the ribbon for her bonnet. It is useless to say she consented. After they had ridden a few miles, she assured the gentleman there was a pasture through which they could drive, which would shorten the road very materially. And the gentleman being very eager to get to the legislative hall, consented to open the gate and drive through, and after driving round and round and gaining no special headway, he at last began to show signs of impatience But the young lady pluckily declared with her sweetest smiles that they would be at the gate in due time, mentally adding:

"At least, as soon as the voting is over in the legislature, and I shall be as glad to be done with my affairs of state as the gentleman will be to begin his— when he reaches the legislative hall this afternoon."

"O, mother, take me, too!"

CHAPTER XXXIV.

THE EIGHT-THOUSAND-DOLLAR BRIBE.

Then Jean thought it time to have a lawyer of her own, and see if there could not be wrung out some justice from the law. She borrowed fifty dollars, which she paid to lawyer Strayton, as a retainer, to secure him against the bribes of her enemies. What a fool! How little she knew of the workings of the law, to think that justice could be bought with so paltry a sum. Only fifty pieces on one side, against fifty thousand on the other. Her lawyer could not have been so easily bought in this case had he not been so poor, and had not his wife sent up such piteous wails that summer, for silk dresses. He was a man of rather fine sympathies, but when he would do good, evil was present with him. He would a little rather do right than wrong when the temptation was not absolutely overpowering. And when Miser and his shaggy-browed counsel offered him three thousand dollars to betray Jean, he at first indignantly spurned them and their gold. Again and again they held up the glittering bait before his hungry eyes, which he as often resolutely resisted; but poverty pressed him on every side; he longed to exchange his humble, unpainted cottage for a grand mansion, with graveled walks. The trial had been put off from time to time in order to let the scandalous stories get well circulated; but at length the time was set again. It was to be a little special court for this case alone, and just three days before the time, Jean's lawyer found he had pressing business at a distance, but called to tell her to be of good cheer; that she would soon have her children; that the case was bound to be decided in her favor, and then she would be rich, as she would certainly get fifteen or twenty thousand dollars with the children for their support. The judge, too, had great respect for him, and anything he might say in her behalf must have its weight, and he would tell a tale of horror that would chill their very heart's blood, and she should go to the court-room and hear the plea. She had not been allowed to know aught of the proceedings, because she was a woman, and her presence in the court-room would be sure to be taken as evidence of her being a coarse, vulgar woman, and so work against her. Her lawyer had insisted all summer, too, that it was so much more modest to have depositions taken, and not bring her witnesses into open court, especially her lady friends. And she afterward found in looking over the records of the case on file in the clerk's office for that county, that her very *honest* and proper attorney must have considered it indelicate to have even the depositions read in court, for she found no record kept of many of the most important ones.

The made-up tales of slander went from mouth to mouth until Jean was in danger of being insulted, and had to keep herself secluded from the lecherous gaze of the idle, pork-and-tobacco-eating, whisky-soaked sensualists that laid around that town.

They could find no one yet base enough to make oath to any of the stories, though they had a rumor of a man living two hundred miles away, who, it was thought, would swear to anything. A desperate struggle must be made by Miser and his counsel to keep the children, as whoever got the children must get the money. So the case was put off again. This new witness was their last refuge; a deputy sheriff was sent in search of him, but when he was found he was too drunk to give his deposition, and when sober he refused to give it.

Jean had grown almost desperate at having the decision put off and put off, and now that they must have a little private court, she could bear it no longer, and told her counsel that immodest or not, she would have some witnesses summoned, gave him the names, and the sheriff, the only *man* in the lot, summoned them to appear on the 29th of November. Some of them lived miles away; still they came early in the morning, but the Court and his friends, not to be thwarted by a little woman, reached the court-house, closed the doors, and proceeded at once to give his decision, so that when her witnesses reached the hall, the judge said he would hear no more testimony, that his mind was already made up.

Yes, Jean feared as much when, on the day before, she saw Miser step into a store opposite her boarding-place, where she knew he had his money on deposit, and come out soon with a portmanteau on his arm, and she knew from the small bulk and great weight hanging down that it was his gold. She watched, with eager eyes; and imagine, if you can, how her heart sank within her, when she saw him walk across the street, and enter the judge's room. She flew into the store to ask the merchant if Miser had taken out his money. He said he had, just that moment. Jean's suspicions were correct. All was lost. She staggered back to her room to find a letter from her lawyer, saying that he could not possibly be present at the trial, as he had bought a lot of hogs on credit, which must be killed immediately and his creditors paid, or he would lose his reputation as an *honest man*. The court-room was crowded with men who had come there mostly to satisfy a morbid curiosity, and though the judge's mind was already "made up," yet that shaggy-browed fiend, Miser's lawyer, Gobbs, stood up in their midst and reiterated all the base slanders that he himself had coined and been the most active in circulating, and abused and defamed Jean, a sick woman, at that time, unable to get off her bed, in the most shameless manner that even a coarse-haired thing in human form could possibly do. The decree of course, was all in favor of the one that carried the purse. No notice was taken of Jean. She had no rights that a man was bound to respect. A divorce was granted Miser, who was to have the children, one a babe, and pay all the costs of court. The Judge, Michael P. Didit, who by the way has since been United States District Judge, a position that the law declares a man shall hold during his life or good behavior, was "dispensing with justice" that year in the Superior Court of Douglas County. He was a coarse, red-haired man, with small eyes, bloated flesh and distended abdomen. He said that Jean had no cause of complaint; that though taken when a mere child and compelled to bear children until broken down in health; though compelled to work hard, and live on a coarse and scanty fare, deprived of the society of civilized people, yet it was within the law; that according to the law a man had a right to marry a child, even at the age of twelve; that the property belongs to the husband, even to the wife's wardrobe, and the money which he got of the missionary for her land was given to him; even her calico dresses, and the bed and fixtures that her mother gave her were to be his; and as for whipping, the law gives the husband reasonable restraint over the wife, in fact he may whip her to death, provided the death don't take place within four days from the whipping. The world is still grieving because Socrates had to drink the poisonous draught, but we think 'twas right for him to bow his head to the decree; for he helped to make the laws of his country, and the law he had helped to enforce against the meanest serf in the country was good enough for him. But God only knows how *hard* it was for Jean to be a law-abiding citizen, and she protested against bending in meek submission to laws she never helped to make. And especially was it *hard*, after lying upon a bed of sickness for months and months, occasioned by her ill-treatment, that took her down to the door of the grave—when pale and trembling she went to see her poor children, and found them in dirt and filth and rags, covered with vermin, their hair matted to their heads by ulcerated sores, to hear their piteous moans for their mother. O, how she wished for power to crush the unequal, man-made laws that thus cruelly trampled on the necks of the innocent and helpless! From time to time she had been to see them since, but could talk with them only as a friend speaks with a friend in prison, under the vigilant eye of a guard. Once she went to see them and found them at a wretched hovel in the midst of squalor and ignorance. The people had instructions not to let her see them at all, and at her approach had secreted them in a dark loft. The coarse, ignorant women were determined that she shouldn't see her children, but she appealed to the man who was working near by, and succeeded not only in gaining his consent, but melted him to tears at the recital of her griefs.

The children were allowed to come out of their gloomy hiding-place. They were overjoyed to meet her, but were compelled to suppress their feelings for fear of being punished. It was a cold, windy, November day, and they were all only half-clad. Her little five-year-old boy had on thin cotton clothes, with great holes worn through at the knees and elbows, his extremities were cold and his frail body chilled through. Jean took him up to her bosom where he nestled as in days of yore, and wept and sobbed as though his little heart would break. Terrified, he told her in whispers how they had taught him that she was a bad woman, that she would steal him, and take him away off and abuse and whip him.

"You wouldn't, mother, would you?" said the child.

"No, my little darling, but they won't let you go with me," said Jean.

Then they both wept together. O, how like breaking her heart-strings it was to go away and leave her children in such a place, and in such a condition as the little boy was, covered from head to foot with the most offensive cutaneous eruptions. When she reached home she sat down and wrote their father a long, touching letter, appealing to his better nature, begging him to use some of his abundant means in the better care of his children, and though they were still kept in ignorance, and poorly clothed and fed, yet she never found them in such destitution and filth as formerly; though she was still prohibited to talk with them, as will be seen by the following card, which appeared in a paper over their father's signature:

"NOTICE.

"Mrs. ———, you are hereby notified to let my children entirely alone. I warn you not to molest or talk to them, or influence them through any other person. The court gave me the exclusive control of said children, and a bill from you. And I further give notice to you to keep off my place and premises at your peril.   O. MISER."

CHAPTER XXXV.

UNDER THE APPLE-TREE BOUGH.

Four years have passed quickly by. Jean has spent them at the Willamette University; the vacations at home with her family, friends and neighbors, with all of whom she is a favorite. At school she has led in every study that she has undertaken. She is a woman at last.

Great God! was there ever such a childhood? The wealth of love and admiration that she meets with everywhere, she drinks in as eagerly as the parched earth drinks up the refreshing shower.

It is vacation now, in August. The summer has been finer than any Italy. To-day has been more than glorious. Jean has been busy helping make pretty linen lawns for her step-sisters, the handsomest girls in the valley, Jean thinks, with their sunny curls, blue eyes and pink-and-white complexions. They are fifteen, eighteen and twenty years of age, now.

The house stands on the same site where their first log-cabin was built. A commodious country frame, with every modern improvement. The whole family have been to supper in the spacious dining-room; the windows are open, and the cool, refreshing sea-breeze is gently toying with the mission rose-bush that stands just outside the window, laden with its wealth of bloom, wafting the delicious fragrance all through the room. The early peaches are ripe, and peaches and cream, with tea, is the charm that induces the family to linger long at the table, until Alfred—the adorable Alfred, a young man now, just nineteen, who can hit the mark every time—says:

"Sis, if we're to bag our game to-night we must

mount and be off; you look so lovely in your new riding habit, I almost wish you were some other fellow's sister."

"Ah, well, Alf," Jean replies with one of her bewitching smiles, as she pokes a long pin through her hat to hold it securely, "I am well satisfied to be yours, for you are the dearest brother a girl ever had."

They galloped along down the lane, over the hills and through the heavy timber. They were a fine couple; Jean on her spirited dapple-gray, and Alfred on his fiery black steed, that took a masterful hand to control. He was eagerly telling her how to take aim, if they spied a deer.

"The deer come out to feed about this time of day," said Alfred.

"It's nearly sundown," Jean said, "I should think; it's getting dark."

"Oh, no, Jean, its only the dense foliage of this tall timber; at noon, some days, it's nearly as dark as night."

"Hark! there are voices," said Jean.

"Yes," answered Alfred, softly, "it is Sis Waldovere and her gentleman friend from San Francisco."

There was a sharp turn in the road, and while he was yet speaking, two people bowed and rode on a few paces. Sis Waldovere drew rein. "Oh, it's you, Alfred, and your sister Jean. It is really getting so dark, and I was so busy talking, I did not recognize you. I was going to send you word that we're all coming over to see you to-morrow."

"At what time?" asked Jean in her flute-like notes.

"Oh, sometime in the forenoon, about eleven o'clock. There are fifteen or twenty of us; look out for danger ahead, Jean," and a little musical laugh went ringing out and echoed back through the woods.

"A magnificent escort Sis Waldovere has to-night. Strange, the best of them can't capture the enchanting Sis."

"He was charming to look at through the bending boughs of that old fir tree that nearly hid him from my view," cried Jean in tones of something like rapture, yet with a little touch of disappointment in them; then with a hum: "The dim old forest, it's quite provoking. It was so near dark I could not see the man. Sis was very much absorbed herself, I think, or she would have seen us sooner."

"Never mind, my dear sister," said Alfred in most pathetic tones, "he will be with the horseback party to-morrow."

They were cantering along and had come out into the open field, where the sun, sure enough, was still shining brightly.

Alfred, glancing at his sister, exclaimed:

"Why, Jean, I never saw you look so lovely. Your eyes are radiant and your lips are cherry red, and a slight flush on cheek and brow—that graceful pose of your lovely neck is like a young fawn's. If I were your lover, I would glide to the ground and swear it was holy, and kneel there forever if you did not bid me rise."

"Why, what a charming lover you would make. I should never believe anyone else as I do you. I think you half in earnest, but a most consummate flatterer. I shall not listen. You will make me silly. No more nonsense; Alf, we must hurry home. You remember Sis's ringing laugh as she started? Well, that was a telegraphic message understood by us girls. It means I must have the house and the girls and everything in "apple-pie" order to-morrow. I must have banks of roses and bloom in every corner of the house, for people take such liberties in an old country house, and they'll wander from garret to cellar. But we'll be ready for them. You'll help me cut flowers in the morning while the dew is on. Those lovely lawn gowns are nearly finished. How glorious for the girls!"

"Aha, Jean, Sis said to you, 'Look out, there is danger ahead!'"

Next morning Jean and the Murdstone girls were up with the larks. The plain, old farm-house was a paradise of bloom; flowers, trailing vines, wild grasses, together with the dark evergreens, made the place enchanting, lovely as a bower, grand as some old cathedral. Jean, in her simple way, had been cultivating her decorative genius all those years in her Umpqua home, and now she had given it free scope, and it was easy for her to take a little insignificant wild flower, and so arrange it with clustering vines and waving grasses that it looked a thing of marvelous beauty. At half past ten the girls were in their pretty lawn gowns, looking from the chamber window for the coming cavalcade of visitors. It was a pretty sight to see so many young men and maidens riding horseback down the long lane. At last, the girls, with rapture, caught sight of them a half a mile away, galloping at full speed. They had just time to clamber hastily down the short flight of stairs, and, with one graceful bound, meet the visitors at the gate—a very pretty, hospitable and comfortable custom in Oregon in those days, and one that ought, by the way, to be preserved by all coming generations in their country homes. The reader will remember that Diogenes demanded this hospitality of his friends, to be met half way. A few of the party went cantering by, the ride being too exhilarating to dismount so soon, but a goodly number, Sis Waldovere among them, were already in the house. Some of the party rambled over the grounds and orchard before entering the house. The introductions took place at the gate. Sis Waldovere never forgot to make everybody acquainted, and set the ball rolling for merriment and laughter. There was always a good time assured when Sis was of the party.

Jean was quite surprised to find that the gentleman she had met riding with Sis Waldovere on the previous evening, was Mr. Reming, the same gentleman who had called at her home in the Umpqua, four years before, with his friend Mr. Stewart. The first words he said to her now were:

"How like your home in the Umpqua! Your individualism expresses itself everywhere alike."

Jean and Mr. Reming had found their way to the old bellflower tree.

And Jean, with a Madonna-like sadness, replied: "How unlike my home in the Umpqua it all is to me."

"That I saw *you* there, surrounded with bloom and wild vines, something like this, is all I remember," persisted Mr. Reming.

"That day will be ever bright in the constellation of memories, Mr. Reming. How I have longed to see you, and tell you what that day has been to me," quietly responded Jean.

Mr. Reming and Sis Waldovere were standing near a pot of wild roses, talking of the beauty of its bloom, when Jean entered, who had been detained telling some of the party where they could find the blackbird's nest, hid in a willow tree that grew on the banks of the Spring branch, just below the orchard. The young birds had abandoned it in the early spring, but the nest remained with some blue-jay's eggs that Alfred had deposited in it to fool the girls, who had gone every day for a week now, to see if the old bird had commenced to hatch her brood.

Jean and Mr. Reming had found their way to the old bellflower tree, whose boughs bent so low under their heavy load of mellow apples that they had to be propped to support the great weight of the golden fruit. Taking one from the bough, Jean handed it to Mr. Reming.

He took it, saying: "I will eat this apple, since it's been held in your fair hand." He pared off its golden coat, letting it fall at his feet, and splitting the apple in two, asked Jean to share it with him.

"Yes, gladly," answered Jean. "this is my favorite apple."

"Do you know if I should ask a woman to share my life with me, I should want her to answer me just as you have now, about the apple. I should want her to say, 'Yes, gladly!'"

Jean, looking down at her pretty shoe plowing its way into the mellow earth, answering, said:

"No doubt she would, if she loved you as I love,"—hesitating a moment, "this apple."

Reming was bending lower to catch the sound of her last word, and looking disappointed, replied:

"My soul was breathlessly waiting to hear 'you' instead of 'apple,' but to-morrow we will probe this question of love and apples still deeper, and you will not say apples then?"

"No," slid from her lips, as easily and naturally as breathing.

Here Sis Waldovere joined them, and they were all moving toward the gate.

Bright glances and sparkling wit had simmered down into cool reasoning over what the entertainment for to-morrow should be, when Sis Waldovere, the adjuster of all differences, proposed they all drive to the Silver Creek Falls. The road was over a delightful country. Everyone was pleased, and Mr. Reming asked Jean to accompany him. The fishing at the Falls for silver trout was enticing, and sure to make the day one of pleasure to them all. The party having enjoyed the ripe, golden apples, picked by fair hands from the heavily laden boughs, and played games of ball with the big red apples, they all assured Jean and the Murdstone girls, they had enjoyed the morning to the full, and mounting their horses, cantered back to the Waldoveres' to partake of dinner.

Mr. Waldovere often entertained twenty or thirty guests at dinner. His house was the center of attraction for years in Oregon, and right royally he could entertain.

When the merry party thronged in, he melted all over in a beaming smile, and with a few cheerful remarks showed them the way to the broad dining-room. The dinner-table was a blaze of beauty. The exquisite perfume of the flowers that ornamented the table so profusely, mingled with the aroma of the fine baked chicken nestling in a fringe of parsley. A finely-baked silver trout floated in a platter of melted, creamy butter; snowy bread and delicious cake threw their incense over the heads of the joyous company, and big rosy apples beamed on the guests as they beamed on each other. The sparkling conversation and brilliant sallies made the occasion ever memorable to the young people, and old Mr. Waldovere even in after years spoke of it with a merry twinkle in his benevolent eye, and with gentle caresses would say to his daughter:

"Well, Sis, it makes me think I'm a boy again to think of that day when Reming came, and you had all been over to see our Jean."

As soon as the guests had all gone, Jean threw herself into a big arm-chair and dreamed the delicious dream of love, and at night when she sought her couch the dream only grew sweeter. The morning dawned upon Jean with bewitching beauty, and so did Mr. Reming with a lovely span of dapple grays. Jean met him at the gate, ready for the ride. She stepped into the buggy and was clasped in the arms that were to enfold her forever. They enjoyed the day as few days were ever enjoyed by mortals on earth. Reming told Jean how he had been detained by his mining interests in California for the last two years; that he had heard from her through his friend Mr. Stewart, and knew she was awaiting his coming.

She told him that the dream of his possible coming had made a twilight for her during the midnight darkness of her deep affliction.

CHAPTER XXXVI.

JEAN STUDYING MEDICINE.

Jean was a woman now, fully equipped for the highest enjoyments of conjugal love. Their engagement was announced to the party as soon as they all assembled at the falls, and the hearty congratulations they received from their merry companions all enhanced the pleasure of the hour. Joy seemed to pervade the whole atmosphere, as the white spray did the air about the falls.

Jean and Mr. Reming were happily married in the fall, and the wedding present that she prized more perhaps than any other was a library containing most of the standard authors, from her husband. The tender companionship of the man she loved, the refined and polished gentleman that ever anticipated her wants, made life so much more to her than it could have been if her soul had not been made so tender and acutely sensitive by the crushing experiences of the past. Though a baby boy, so promising and bright, was followed in seasonable time, by a little girl,—the fair-haired Dot, that the reader will remember having been mentioned in the opening chapter—yet the deep, longing mother love for her babies in the woods drove the mother-heart to some deeds of daring that were rather unusual for a woman. She determined to write a story, and this required some preparation to fit herself for so arduous an undertaking; she must, at least, master some of the sciences, especially that of medicine.

At that date, in '68, a woman had never been permitted to enter the sacred precincts of a medical college on the Pacific Coast, and it was possible that they would not be admitted for many years to come. Here was an obstacle that must be met and overcome. Jean and Mr. Reming had many friends in the Willamette University, and as that institution had just added a department of medicine to its curriculum, Jean and her husband interviewed a few of the trustees and professors—noble-souled men, who said she should enter as a student if she so desired. They, with their big, common-sense, Pacific Coast brains, said they did not know why women should not learn medicine as well as their a b c's.

Everything being arranged, it was announced by one of the professors in a daily paper that a woman had applied for admittance into the medical college and been admitted. Everybody was on the tiptoe of curiosity as to who she could be and where she was to come from. At the opening of the term, everybody was charmed and delighted, and thought it the most appropriate thing in the world, when the door was opened and our dauntless Jean passed in and took the place of preference that had been assigned her, just in front of the professor, who was already discoursing upon anatomy; and the young students, half shame-faced and apologetical, took the earliest opportunity to assure her that they had not the remotest idea that it could be she, or they never should have passed a resolution attempting to exclude her from their class. Jean passed the entire term in the society of the professors and young gentlemen students, no other woman entering the hall the whole term, so much prejudice existed in the outside circles against women studying medicine. Jean, however, was too much absorbed in her studies to observe this, or even miss them. She never lost a day, and scarcely an hour, and the professors remarked that she was more punctual in attendance than any man among them. There was never a word uttered, either, by professor or student, during the whole term, that might not with perfect propriety have been spoken in any parlor in Christendom, and the students declared that they had made more rapid progress with their studies this year than ever before, because they had wasted no time in the usual larks and story-telling common to medical students. They seemed supremely satisfied with themselves, and never wanted to be in a medical college again without a woman student in it; and their wish has been gratified, as women have been in attendance every term since. No band of brothers could have been more courteous, considerate or helpful, than this band of students were during the three years that Jean was in attendance at the college. After spending three years in the Willamette University, Jean went to New York and had the benefit of attending the hospitals and lectures, and was graduated with honors in '72 from the Women's Medical College.

Jean, having spent many years on the Pacific Coast, and traveled over thousands of miles of the richest and most productive soil, that only needed the magic touch of the husbandman to make it yield everything necessary to the growth and sustenance of a densely populated country, and seeing it wholly uninhabited save by wild Indians and herds of buffalo, it only required a visit to the overcrowded cities of the East to see at once the necessity of making the people understand that they could make homes in the far West, and be infinitely happier and better surrounded than they could ever hope to be in the eastern states.

It is the legitimate business of a true physician to feel the needs of the people and seek to benefit them. In spending the winter of 1872 in New York City completing her medical studies, Jean was brought into immediate contact with many of the poor, living in tenement houses, as well as in the hospitals; and it did not take a very comprehensive mind to see how much better off those people would be were they scattered over the broad country of the Pacific Coast. Jean had a millionaire brother-in-law, Mr. Barron, in whose home she was surrounded with all the privileges and advantages of wealth, and from this home and social standpoint she saw much of the elegance and culture, refinement and splendor of New York's wealth.

Poor old Horace Greeley's "Go West, young man, go West," was ringing out upon the ears of an awakening people, who are just now beginning to put his idea into practice. Grant was at the zenith of his glory; Sumner was the great statesman in the United States Senate; Roscoe Conkling, the leading politician of the Republican party; Wm. H. Vanderbilt, the towering millionaire and railroad king, was just then beginning to grasp the control of his father's colossal fortune, young, strong, manly, clear-headed, with honest purpose to do right.

It was Jean's extreme good fortune to meet those gentlemen quite often during her stay in New York, and at the capitol. One Sunday morning, when Henry Ward Beecher was addressing a large concourse of people in the Academy of Music in New York city, there being no space in the vast auditorium, Jean was, along with others, compelled to stand on the platform and listen to the smooth, flowing eloquence of the speaker, charmed with the voice and gesture of the great man, but woefully disappointed in the matter of his discourse. He was graphically portraying the homes of the American people. Perhaps no person upon whose ear the voice of the great man fell that day, was more strongly moved to act upon what he had left unsaid, than the little woman from far beyond the Rockies. He did not speak of the Pacific Coast, nor the grand possibilities of this vast and then almost unknown territory. Afterward, Jean had occasion to speak to him about this sermon delivered at the Academy of Music in New York, to more people, it seemed to her, than lived on the Pacific Coast at that time. She told him the music of his voice, the poetry of his gestures, the magnetism of his mighty genius were all lost on her because he left out our whole country—that portion, she told him, that was to be the balance of power of the civilized world, and he did not mention it.

"I know it is great; I feel its coming power, but," said he, "that is your province; tell the people of it. I cannot, I never saw it; but in God's good time, I will. I can feel the beauty, the vastness of its plains, the grandeur of its mountains, the goodness of its soil, just by looking at you. Come to my house and tell me all about it."

"Ah! if I had your oratory, your audience," she said.

"I am like a canary bird, caged," said Mr. Beecher.

"You look to me more like a lion," was Jean's laughing rejoinder.

"Use a pen and the press, madame, said he, "and your audience will be millions, where mine are only thousands."

Imbued with a strong purpose, bowing low, she said, "I will write for the people." That afternoon, before her indignation had cooled, she wrote a paper on the chances for home-building on the Pacific coast. And one of the first lines was, "What a pity our forefathers had not planted their feet on Pacific soil instead of on Plymouth Rock." She contrasted our climate with theirs on the bleak Atlantic side, and told them they would never have to put earth on the sunny side of a rock to grow a hill of corn, as they do in New Hampshire and Vermont, if they lived in California. As the paper was quite lengthy, she rolled it up and tied it about with a blue ribbon,* and walked from 227 Lexington avenue to the new railroad depot, and was ushered into the presence of the great railroad king, Wm. H. Vanderbilt. At eleven o'clock on Sunday, Jean was listening to the discourse on homes; before eleven o'clock on Monday morning she was reading an argument to Wm. H. Vanderbilt that clinched his convictions that the fare on the one line of cars then crossing the continent was much too high, and must be reduced.

* The great temperance cause had not then made it an emblem.

"If one hundred people pay two hundred and fifty dollars apiece, the income into the company's treasury will not be so large a sum as one thousand people carried for one hundred dollars apiece. Also, the increase of freight is an immense item, when the increase of travel is considered. The railroad company must see the great advantage if the question is fairly brought before them, Mr. Vanderbilt."

"I will see to that," said he. "Will you take this article to Mr. Greeley, tell him you read it to me, and that I want it published in the New York *Tribune?* It is the best article ever written for our railroads, Madam. Where have you lived all this time, that I never heard of you before?"

"I was born in this state, sir, but have lived nearly all my life on the Pacific Coast, and am thoroughly conversant with the country, its immense possibilities, its pressing needs. What we want is people. It takes people to build cities, towns, and develop new countries."

"I know it," said he, "and I have been trying to get railroad men to reduce the fare to the Pacific Coast, but heretofore they would not listen. I will give you the names of four leading railroad men. You see them and talk to them as you have to me. They will read this in the *Tribune,* and at our next meeting of the directors in two weeks, I will do all I can to have the fare reduced one half to the Pacific Coast, and," added he, with a complacent smile, "I think I have some influence with railroad men."

The great railroad magnate, evidently not being willing to ask favors without conferring greater, took a small card—a pass to the Pacific Coast—and writing her name and his own upon it, handed it to her, saying:

"Madam, as long as you wish it, you shall travel free on any railroad or steamer line while you write such articles as that."

Jean being unsophisticated in railroad passes, and thinking she was not ready to go, handed the card back. By the pleased and puzzled smile upon his countenance, it must have been a new experience, and he returned the card to her, remarking:

"You had better keep it."

Jean glanced at it with new interest, and found it to be good for a year.

Jean saw Mr. Greeley; he looked at the paper and said: "Madam, you're a writer; this shall be published, and we should be pleased to secure you as a correspondent from the Pacific Coast for the *Tribune*." The fare was reduced at the next directors' meeting, one-third, not one-half, as the mighty railroad magnate said it should be. However, they were greatly rejoiced at that reduction, as people soon began to come in much larger numbers, and the increase in travel was great in proportion; being now, according to railroad statistics, not less than 150,000 yearly.

There never was a time in the history of a nation when the permanent prosperity of a people seeking new homes was so secure as on the Pacific Coast at the present time. The railroad facilities are something prodigious, there being at present networks of railroads spanning the country, hither and thither, every prominent point boasting of its railroad center.

This gives the home-seeker a chance to see the advantage of all points. He can build him a home by the sea, or perch on a mountain-top, nestle in a valley or spread himself all over a vast plain—if he has money enough. He can find a snug little spot shut in and surrounded by lofty mountains, or buy a ranch and stake out a town, sell lots and build himself a city according to his own liking. This has been done inside of a year; but if one cares only for building himself a home, he can see the whole country thousands of miles, in a month's time, of the choicest land under the sun, with the best climate in the world, and in another month's time he can build him a residence in the latest style, with every modern improvement. He can find in this country some of the best architectural designs to choose from that his purse or good taste may dictate, and in six months, green lawns, and flowers that bloom the year round, with rare tropical plants, will beautify the grounds; and in a short time his happiness and success will permeate every letter he writes home until not a long time will elapse when he will have all his best friends and neighbors around him, enjoying the delightful sensation of living in a new world of his own making.

CHAPTER XXXVII.

INTERVIEWING MR. GREELEY.

When Jean called at the Union Square League Rooms, she sent her card in to the editor of the New York *Tribune*. On it was written: "Jean Reming, Salem, Oregon," with "Pacific Coast" in the corner, to insure her being properly placed in the world.

The great man, who was a few days after nominated for the presidency on the Democratic ticket, soon strode into the gorgeous apartment that Jean had been ushered into when the young man assured her Mr. Greeley was in, and would see her soon. Jean was reveling in the beauty of the building; the wealth and grandeur of its furniture, carpets, draperies, pictures, statuary, everything was engrossing her attention, when the great man entered, walking like one absorbed in thought. His manner was refined, graceful, self-possessed, with an air of amiable serenity, characteristic of great men; but there was a pink flush upon his face that spoke to the little woman of science, too much nervous excitement for healthy conditions; otherwise, a remarkably well-preserved man of ripe years. He was well dressed, but plain, quiet, and scrupulously neat, there being nothing conspicuous about his dress, excepting that his huge feet were incased in a rather coarse, broad shoe that looked out of place in such a place as the Union Square League Rooms, but would, our Jean thought, be a perfection of comfort and appropriateness in a corn-field. He bowed, looking at Jean's card, and pointed to a seat near him while seating himself. Then the questions opened fire and the sparks flew on both sides. Jean had no favors to ask, no fears to control. Two freer or more untrammeled brains never met to discuss the living issues of the day. The great philosopher said he was pleased to meet a woman so well versed on the questions of such interest to the people and so conversant with the Pacific Coast. But when she said, "what a pity, Mr. Greeley, our forefathers had not planted their feet on Pacific soil instead of on Plymouth Rock;" then a battle of words ensued, and Mr. Greeley rose and walked the floor and put his fingers through his thin locks. "Warm climates make people lazy and indolent, like the people down South," said he. "Is the South anything compared to the North? This country would never have been anything had it not been for the severe climate that drove men to work like heroes to save them from its inclemency. It is the making of the world that it is compelled to struggle."

"Yes, Mr. Greeley, you can tell that to these people, but not to me, who have lived on the Pacific Coast, and know where a people can work the whole year round, never stopping for frost or snow, or blizzards, and where the trees and grain and vegetables grow the whole year round, that the opportunities are better for the welfare of the people and for growing rich than where they are interrupted so often. Was there ever another spot on the earth where people have progressed as rapidly as on the Pacific Coast? Was there ever a city built so thoroughly, rapidly and magnificently as San Francisco? The climate evidently is not warm enough to make the people indolent there, Mr. Greeley."

"Yes, but it was the gold mines that built San Francisco."

"No matter what helped to build it, Mr. Greeley, it stands as a monument of Pacific Coast pluck, energy and ability, and didn't it take pluck and energy to dig the gold from the mines, Mr. Greeley? They grow from fifty to sixty bushels of wheat to the acre. Doesn't that require some energy? I see that our white wheat brings the highest market price in London and New York. Doesn't it take some ability to do that?

"Are you sure," asked Mr. Greeley, "that your figures are correct about growing fifty or sixty bushels of wheat to the acre?"

"Yes," answered Jean, "I have measured it with my own hands, and sold it for five dollars a bushel in '51 and '52, and under such circumstances, I would be likely to know."

Mr. Greeley remarked: "You're a writer, madam; we want you as correspondent from the Pacific Coast, giving us accounts of its products, climate, soil and its possibilities for home-making."

Jean accepted the proposition, and was duly installed as correspondent from the Pacific Coast to the *New York Tribune.*

Jean then told him about her interview with Wm. H. Vanderbilt, and that he had promised to reduce the fare from New York to San Francisco. Greely replied that he was glad, as the fare had been absolutely exorbitant from the first.

"I should think that if you had used your influence toward getting the rates reduced, it would have been a greater inducement for the people to go West than your advice to go West."

Mr. Greely, with a quizzical smile, asked: "Why don't you ask me if I'm in favor of woman's suffrage? All the other women do. You are working like a man, and accomplishing your work. You are getting enough support from us men to carry your points, and you haven't said anything about woman's rights, either. You have brought the biggest questions that ever a women asked me to aid her in, and I have promised the support of the *Tribune,* before you ask for it, and will not go back on my word."

"Yes, but, Mr. Greeley, I have asked the support of Mr. W. H. Vanderbilt, and ask yours now, in getting a land law passed, giving women a right to take up government land for homesteads the same as men, and I want the *Tribune* to give the question the strongest support that it can."

"Have you read the Almanac?" inquired Mr. Greeley.

"Read the Almanac?" queried Jean. "What could the Almanac do toward inducing the government to pass a land law for women?" and she looked with her scientific eye into the face of the philosopher, thinking his political aspirations had turned his head a little. Then in a high key almost akin to a whine, he said:

"*My* Almanac; I have published the land laws in it, and if you have not read it, you get one and read it."

"Oh, yes, since you've mentioned it, I remember to have read it thoroughly, and it stirred my temper to think the government would give all the land to its men and none to its women."

And Mr. Greeley said:

"Of course, it's a great injustice."

Jean Reming said she thought she had influence enough to go to Washington and get the bill passed. That Mr. Vanderbilt had promised to write to Senator Conkling, who was at that time perhaps the most influential man in the Senate.

Mr. Greely then said he had been invited to talk to the State Agricultural Society, in Cooper Institute, two weeks from that time, and if she would prepare a paper on the Pacific Coast, and consent to come and read it, he would be glad to introduce her. Jean could not promise until she had consulted some of her friends. Her ambitious friends decided, however, that it was an opportunity she could not afford to decline, and she wrote Mr. Greeley she would be prepared.

CHAPTER XXXVIII.

INTRODUCED BY MR. GREELEY TO THE AGRICULTURAL SOCIETY, COOPER INSTITUTE, NEW YORK CITY.

At the appointed time, after listening to the thrilling eloquence and stirring truths of what Mr. Greeley knew about agriculture and the welfare of the people, Jean Reming, with her paper in hand, was introduced to the audience.

Mr. Greeley had made the remark, in his speech, that if any *man* told them that they could go to the Pacific Coast and raise stock during winter, without food or shelter, that they could say to the man "You lie."

The first words that Jean uttered were:

"I am glad that Mr. Greeley has left a chance for a *woman* to say that she has lived on the Pacific Coast for twenty years, her family having been stock raisers, and that the cattle had been fat and sleek all winter with no other shelter than the broad-spreading forests afford, and no other food than the wild luxuriant grasses."

The audience here applauded to the echo, proving that they believed what was being told them.

Jean had clipped a few items from the army reports of the old Indian fighter, General Harney, where he said they had gone into camp late in November, with their horses thin and tired out, and turned them all out on the wild grasses, and they were rolling-fat in the spring, ready for marching. Then she read quite a lengthy paper about crossing the plains and the grandeur of the Pacific coast. This is the paper:

"Having come east this fall to complete my medical studies, while in attendance at the colleges and hospitals, mingling with the people, I necessarily come in contact with the two extremes of labor and capital, poverty and wealth. The ignorance of the people in reference to our glorious country, and their eagerness to become acquainted with it, are equally remarkable. They know something of California, but Oregon and Washington are mythlands they never heard of—though when it comes to 'Pugget Sound,' as they call it, they can enlighten me, especially the railroad men. I find the people eager, anxious and hungry for information, and am importuned on all sides, particularly by women. After living so long in the Pacific wilds, I am alike anxious to get a peep into the mysteries of your great city and feel its throbbing pulse. I have visited the factories and workshops where thousands of unmarried women are employed. I must wear about me a Pacific Coast air, for wherever I go women seem to instinctively recognize me as coming from the Pacific Coast. Their questions are so many and varied, that in private conversation to answer them all, would be a greater task than I care to undertake, even for the sake of my much-loved section and the enlightenment of my fellow-women, for whom I feel willing to make any reasonable sacrifice. So I consented to accept an invitation from the Hon. Horace Greeley, who is a candidate for the Presidency, to meet him and you in Cooper Institute, and in a brief address give you a few facts in regard to our country and some of its capabilities, the hardships that the pioneers endured, with the present easy facilities for making the trip across the plains. Now we can ride in palace cars, on cushioned seats, and be whirled across the continent in the incredibly short space of seven days.

"Years ago, before the Union Pacific was thought of, the stalwart, sturdy men of the West — the bravest, grandest men that ever did a noble act—huddled their women and children into ox-wagons, taking with them bread, beans and bacon for a six months' trip. The starting-point for these pioneers was on the banks of the Missouri river, opposite St. Joseph. Here they organized into companies of two or three hundred, for mutual protection against the hostilities of the Indians through whose almost unexplored territories they had to pass. At this point of the Missouri river they bade farewell to their homes, government, friends and civilization, and moved on with slow and steady march to the goal of their destination—the glorious sunset land bordering on the Pacific Coast. The land of towering mountains, big trees and delightful valleys, where the flowers bloom every month in the year; where the sleek cattle feed all the year round, without thought of shelter other than the broad-spreading forests afford. Here they came and took possession of the virgin soil and inherited it; they and their sons and their daughters, under the flag, forever. They were as dead to the friends left behind, who had scarce a faint hope of ever hearing of them again alive. And should they be murdered by the Indians it would be only by the merest chance they would ever hear of it. Mothers folded their little ones to their breasts and silently offered a prayer to that God who led Moses through the wilderness to the promised land. Men, with a sharp crack of their bull-whips, cried in a loud, clear tone: 'Whoah, haw! whoah, haw!' to the mute brutes by their sides, to prove to each other, and their own hearts, too, that they were as unfaltering as their voices.

"These journeys were usually commenced about the first of April, and if no serious delay occurred, ended about the last of October or late in November; but now and then a belated party was overtaken by the deep snows in the mountains, and of course, all perished.

"These were trips to try men's souls, and, under the most favorable circumstances, glorious for developing pluck in a fellow. Woe! to the poor craven who started without a good supply. He might as well have forgotten his bacon and beans or his bowie-knife. There were mountains to climb where team after team of oxen must be doubled to pull up one wagon. There were huge points of rock to be clambered round, over which men joined hands and literally carried the wagons. There were steep mountain sides to go down, where the wagons were lowered by ropes; there were wild, roaring, rapid rivers to be crossed, with wagon beds corked tight for boats. There were bridges to build, forests to fell to make passes through mountain gorges. There were midnight vigils to keep, standing guard, for the Indians to shoot or scalp you just as they chose. Vast herds of wild buffalo came thundering over the plains with their thick short horns and shaggy manes, and their tails raised high in air just as you have seen them in the pictures. They must be warded off from making a charge right through their ranks and stampeding the cattle. There were matinees and evening concerts given free of charge by prowling wolves, whose faintest howl would send the soul of a coward shivering to his boots. There were marches to be made, over sands too hot for man or beast under the scorching rays of a noon-day sun, and so must be made in the cool of the evening and through the long night.

"I well remember one of these long marches. Sometimes they lasted for days without water, except that we carried with us in casks. My father crossed the plains twenty years in advance of the Union Pacific Railroad, and he vowed that for the accommodation of his wife and little ones, he would stick to the family carriage and his tried and trusty horses until the Indians stole them. On this occasion, when the men were worn out with fatigue and loss of sleep, several of them sickened and could hold out no longer, and here the women came to the rescue. I was, at that time, a mere child. The reins of the old family carriage were, with its precious freight, intrusted to my care. I had held the reins and guided them with safety over difficult places, in the day-time, but to take charge of them at night, lighted save by a dim starlight over a trackless road, all untried for a year, required a piece of masterly skill that I would have gladly resigned to some masculine hand. Father said: 'Courage, my child,' as he handed me the reins, 'the horses know your voice, and will obey your lightest touch. They'll keep the road. Hold a tight rein when you go down a steep place—that's all. The men are awfully sick, and I am afraid one poor fellow will die before morning.'

"I did hold a tight rein and trusted in God and the horses, and must have had a little faith in my own puny strength, by the way I braced my feet and pulled back as we went down the steep places.

"I remember, too, how the encouraging words of our brave captain cheered us as he rode back and forth along the lines, and how eagerly the almost famished cattle would have rushed headlong down the mountain side, when they came in sight of the winding river that lay in the dim distance below. Thus we traveled on, constantly meeting new dangers and surmounting new difficulties, though on the way we crossed rolling prairies where the sweet grasses grew luxuriantly. I gathered the pretty wild flowers and twined them in wreaths for my hair as I saw the Indian maidens do. We were beguiled by the song of birds, fragrance of fair flowers, the balmy air, and the clear, cool waters of the pebbly brooks; and such a sky! with its many-tinted fleecy clouds. We were many times compelled to acknowledge that this was more like paradise than anything we had hoped to find on earth, and yet we could not tarry long to enjoy these scenes, for this was the hunting-ground of many valiant Indian tribes who were at that time untainted by civilization, or we could never have passed through their country unmolested, killing their game; and leaving destruction in our wake. For our hunters, with unerring aim, took pride in bringing down their game: the buffalo, the monarch of the plain; the fleet-footed deer, the bright-eyed antelope, sage hen and squirrel, nor sometimes, I fear, left unharmed the sociable and amiable little prairie-dog.

"My mother, a woman of forty, and I, a mere child, would often sit down to rest, philosophize and feast on the beauties around us. We would select building sites just where we would like to live all our days if there were only people enough to take possession and hold it. People enough to take possession and hold it—'Ay! there's the rub.' Now, Mr. Greeley says, the people won't go and live in isolated homes. He has been telling them to go West all along, but they won't do it. They want to be pent up and crowded in these great cities. A finer truth he never spoke. People do want to be crowded. I own I want to be crowded a little myself. I have had too much elbow-room all my life on the Pacific Coast. What we need is people to come in crowds, in flocks, like birds migrating. What could *one* man do all alone on a sand-bar in the middle of the Pacific Ocean? What success would Mr. Greeley have with his printing-press out West a hundred miles from everybody else. What could he have done right here on Manhattan Island two hundred years ago. It takes people to build cities and develop the resources of a country. I am a native of New York State, but the Pacific Coast is the land of my adoption. I love it for its just and equal laws, for its recognition of the claims of women. Men cannot help but be brave and gallant and just, who breathe such pure air and look upon such grand and sublime scenery! I know what a fine thing it is for women to own land in their own right. I was one of those fortunate women who held three hundred and twenty acres of land under the donation act of 1851. I have seen the good effects of that law among my countrywomen. I have seen reckless husbands squandering in bad speculations all their acres, broken and disheartened with their misfortunes, move right over to the wife's half section, which was sacred from the rude touch of the sheriff, and commence life anew in the cultivation of the soil, feeling that somehow it was right after all that the old bird should be mistress of her own nest.

"One of the faults of the donation act was that it did not extend over a long-enough term of years. Such a law in all the territories to-day would open up the millions of wild acres faster than railroads, and the land wouldn't all fall into the hands of greedy corporations. The act expired, I think, in 1858, just about the time people began to find out there was such a law. If there is anything really obscure on earth, that does not shed one ray of light on the people, it is some of the enactments of Congress. I believe we were more hopeful then of the country's rapid settlement than we are to-day. And again, by the telegraph wire we heard the sound of the last stroke that connected the East, with its toiling millions, with the mighty West. Our heart-beats quickened as we thought of the beautiful homes, thriving villages and growing cities that would spring up, before the smoke of the wigwam scarcely died; and after waiting and wondering why the people did not come, we consoled ourselves by thinking our land was so delightful it was like that other 'bourne from whence no traveler returns'—a land of gold, sunshine and showers; where the brave free spirits are; where the green sward of the fields and the groves afford a soft carpet for our feet; where flowers spring up as thick as the stars of heaven, all bespangled with the heavy dews of evening; where the big red apples grow; where the rich, mellow earth yields its sixty or seventy-five bushels of wheat to the acre, and where, if our eastern farmers could be transplanted, they would think they were in the Garden of Eden; where the mountains climb higher, with their eternal snow caks nearer the throne of Him who spoke them into being. Our rivers are deeper, swifter and clearer, and afford us purer and colder water to drink, fresh from the snowy mountains, than any in the world, to say nothing of the innumerable springs that bubble up at intervals all over the land. Were there ever finer facilities offered for farms? There is room enough in the valleys of the Willamette, Sacramento and San Joaquin to supply a million people with better facilities for living than the same space east of the Rocky Mountains. Our rivers afford such excellent mill privileges; and then our inexhaustible forests of fir, pine and cedar, oak, ash and maple. Why, the staunchest ships that sail the seas will yet be built from the timber of these forests. Ships that will sail in and out of our peaceful harbors laden with the wealth of the world. And such a climate! with the rolling hills, the undulating valleys, the cool nights, the bracing air, and pure water, the very sanitarium of the nation. It can never be unhealthful there! And only to think how the poor farmers down-east have to work enriching and recuperating their exhausted soil with gypsum, and bringing whole ship-loads of guano from the islands of the Pacific, and building stone fencing round stony farms, making room on the little patches here and there to grow a meager subsistence. Why, I have heard them tell of putting earth on the sunny side of a rock to grow a hill of corn! In our county they would have nothing to do but to plow the ground, sow the seed, and reap the golden harvest. I have taken up the dear earth in my hand and examined it, to see if it was really just such soil as grew the brightest flowers at home in my corner of the garden.

"I have laid my heart on the bosom of old mother earth and wept like a tired child on its mother's breast; not because I had conquered it, and there were no more conquests to make, as Alexander did; but because the ground was lying idle there that should yield such harvests to the people, and they crowded here in the great cities, starving to death, slowly starving, yet none the less surely, while hundreds of thousands of acres of arable land are only waiting to be tilled by the husbandman, to yield the richest reward.

"In the name of humanity why don't Congress donate these lands to the half-fed millions toiling in the great cities for barely bread enough to keep their souls in their bodies, and make an appropriation, if necessary, to assist these miserable poor in getting on to these lands! As a question of economy, is it not cheaper to place men and women on a firm basis where they can make their own living, than to keep them crowded together, overworked and half-starved until out of sheer desperation they commit some crime and then shut them up to punish them.

"Some one has said: 'It costs more to catch one thief, convict and thoroughly punish him than to feed twenty honest men.'

"Society and the churches are doing a noble work in gathering up the poor little unfortunates, building immense charity-homes, educating and trying to save them from the evil influences that are forever contaminating the good there is in the innocence of childhood, saving them out of the miry cesspools of our great cities; and yet this loving charity is not deep enough to quite reach the case as our innumerable prison-pens do testify. The wise Channing has said:

"'There is a duty higher than to build alms-houses for the poor, and that is to save men from being degraded to the blighting influence of an alms-house.' And the way to save men is to give them plenty of room on God's broad earth. If a hundred and sixty acres won't allure them, give them three hundred and twenty. That will redeem, elevate, ennoble and save them from gaunt misery and disease, from moral turpitude, and crimes more horrible to endure than death itself. Why should human beings be pent up in these large cities, like cattle in a pen, fed on husks, when there is plenty in their father's household and they know it? We boast of our charities while we are stealing all the roseate glow of health from the cheeks of youth and beauty, crushing out all the energies of ambitious youth and prostrating the towering strength of manhood.

Many a brave and noble fellow has escaped this fate by going West; but alas! he has had to bear the heartache of a life all alone. Many a sweet, pure girl, with the silvery threads creeping into her once golden-brown curls, is sighing and saying, 'Ah me! he is gone.' And if ever those waiting, longing, loving souls should meet the brave fellows beyond the Rocky Mountains, will not the hill-tops and valleys resound to the heart-throbbing raptures of love? I do not believe that God ever intended that so many men should live on the Pacific Coast without wives, and so many women here without husbands. The men want wives to share with them the wealth and grandeur and happiness that is in store there for all who work for it."

Thus Jean closed her speech, and if the sea of upturned faces were eager before, they were clamorous now. Where they asked one question before, they asked a hundred now, and for one invitation to lecture she now received fifty. Their attention was awakened and their inquisitiveness aroused; and letters came pouring in by the hundreds. Jean sent the letters all off to the Oregon Legislature then in session. The question of immigration came up after her return, and a bill was introduced to encourage it. By a unanimous vote, Jean Reming was elected Immigration Commissioner, with a small salary. These letters attracted the attention of the business men, who saw the necessity of organizing immigration bureaus.

CHAPTER XXXIX.

IN THE UNITED STATES SENATE.

Before Jean's return to California, she went to Washington, interviewed President Grant, Senators Conkling, Sumner, and a perfect constellation of brilliant minds that were assembled at that time in the Senate of the United States. And in five days' time she had the following land bill for women, before it was revised or amended, drawn up and introduced by Senator Kelly of Oregon, and had been invited by the Senate Committee on Public Lands to come before it and make her claim. She afterward learned that she was the first woman ever invited to speak before one of the congressional committees. The speech must have been somewhat thrilling and pathetic, as when she had finished there was not a dry eye among the senators, and a tear glistened on her own lids. However, she was successful, and the bill was reported favorably to the Senate.

IN THE SENATE OF THE UNITED STATES, MAY 4, 1872.

Mr. Pomeroy, from the committee on Public Lands, reported the following bill which was read the first and second times and recommitted to the committee on Public Lands.

A bill, supplementary to an act entitled "*An act to secure homesteads to actual settlers on the public domain.*"

Be it enacted by the Senate and House of Representatives of the United States of America in Congress assembled, that every woman, whether married or single, now residing in the State of Oregon, or in any one of the territories of the United States, or who shall, hereafter become such resident and who is and shall become a citizen of the United States, shall, upon complying with the provisions of this act, or the act to which it is supplementary, be entitled to a tract of land, not exceeding one quarter-section, of one hundred and sixty acres of the public lands, subject to preemption or private entry in such state or territory in which she may reside.

Sec. 2. That in order to entitle any woman mentioned in the preceding section to such tract of land, she shall reside upon and cultivate the same for four consecutive years, or, in lieu of such residence and cultivation, she shall reside two years in the state or territory in which the land is situate, and make, or cause to be made, improvements on such tract of the value of two hundred dollars, by erecting buildings and fences, or by clearing and cultivating the same. Instead of acquiring title to such land in either of the modes herein before prescribed, she may do so by paying to the receiver of the proper land-office the sum of one dollar for each acre of such tract of land, after becoming a resident of said state or territory in which the land is situate.

Sec. 3. That any woman, desirous of acquiring a title to land, under the provisions of this act, may, at any time after she becomes a resident of said state, or of either of said territories, make application in writing to the register of the land-office in the district where the lands are situate, setting forth the manner in which she proposes to acquire title to the same, and specifying the particular legal subdivision of land which she claims; and she shall also state in her application that the said land is for her exclusive use and benefit, and not, either directly or indirectly, for the benefit of any other person or persons whomsoever, and such application shall be verified by her oath or affirmation. Upon proving to the satisfaction of the register and the receiver of the proper land-office, by two credible and disinterested witnesses, and also by the affidavit of the claimant, that she has complied with the requirements of this act, so far as residence and cultivation, or residence and improvements, are concerned, or upon the payment to the receiver of one dollar per acre for such land, she shall be entitled to a patent certificate from the register and the receiver for the tract of land specified in her application; and if the same shall be approved by the Commissioner of the General Land Office, she shall be entitled to a patent, in her own right, for such tract of land. And if she be a married woman such land shall not be liable to be sold upon execution, or in any way disposed of to pay the debts or liabilities of her husband.

SEC. 4. That in case of the death of any woman who shall have filed her application, and commenced proceedings to obtain a title to a tract of land as hereinbefore provided, before she shall have complied with the requirements of this act, all her rights shall descend to her heirs at law, unless she shall otherwise dispose of the same by will, executed according to the laws of the state or territory where she resided; and proof of residence and cultivation upon the land, up to the time of her death, shall be sufficient to entitle them to a patent for the same. But if the decedent shall not have made, or caused to be made, the improvements, or paid the money herein required, it shall be lawful for such heirs or devisees, or the executor or administrator of the estate of such decedent, to make the improvements or pay the money to the receiver as specified in this act; and thereupon such heirs or devisees shall be entitled to a patent certificate for the tract of land.

SEC. 5. That if, at any time after filing her application as required by this act, any woman entitled to the benefits of this law shall cease to reside upon and cultivate the land claimed by her for the period of six months at any one time, she shall forfeit all her right to the same, and such land shall revert to the United States; or if any such woman shall fail to make the improvements herein required upon the land claimed in her application, or pay the money for such land for the period of one year after filing the same, then all her rights to the same shall become forfeited and the land revert to the United States.

SEC. 6. That no woman shall be permitted to acquire title to more than one quarter-section of land under the provisions of this act; and the commissioner of the General Land Office is hereby required to prepare and issue such rules and regulations, consistent with this act, as shall be necessary and proper to carry its provisions into effect; and where not otherwise provided in this act, he shall be governed by the provisions of the act to which this is supplementary, so far as the same are applicable.

While Jean was at the capitol, a funny little incident, that has never yet been in print, occurred in consequence of Jean's not understanding the full force of our democratic-republicanism. She supposed that greatness would demand some pomp and ceremony, even in free America. Something of hero-worship, or servitude of kingcraft, or something of that kind, must have taken possession of her mind, as she was fully imbued with the idea that to insure an introduction to the president some senator must introduce her. She accordingly selected Senator Conkling as the most fitting person perhaps in the whole senate for so arduous an undertaking, since she had had a letter of introduction to Senator Conkling that Mr. Vanderbilt had promised to send her, and had already had a moment's conference with the great senator. It happened that day that Jean had prepared her toilet with extraordinary care. It was the morning when Conkling was fighting the meanness of some small men who were opposed to giving government land to maimed soldiers. His words were hurled like an avalanche, burying his opponents under the debris of his contempt, forever out of sight, or any fear that their little vote would damage anybody ever again; certainly not the brave defenders of our glorious country who had lost an arm or a leg in defense of our homes.

Jean was carried away with his eloquence, and when his speech was ended, she sent him her card by the page, not knowing that he had to give his entire attention to the intrigue of his opponents; supposing when his speech was ended there was nothing else to do, and he could now turn his whole ability to introducing her to the President of the United States. It was the greatest occasion of her life; she was overwhelmed with enthusiasm, listening to the glowing words of the man fighting for the rights of his fellowmen; she would espouse the cause of her sisters, and fight as courageously and well.

When Jean sent her card, the page entered a mild protest, saying the senator was very much engaged. Jean insisted, and the page very quietly laid the card on the senator's desk. Conkling took no notice; he was looking a thunderbolt across at a senator who was inquiring how a man with only one arm or leg could cultivate the soil? Jean was disheartened; she wondered if such creatures would pop up in the Senate-chamber and ask if it was possible for women to chop down trees or plow a field? She was becoming restless, and wanted to see the noble Grant. She was sure he would indorse the land law for women. She sent on another card and another; it fluttered to the floor. Conkling caught the name as the page replaced it on the desk; he listened to the boy, who told him where the lady sat waiting. She had a position behind a curtain where, unobserved, she could survey the whole floor of the Senate-chamber, and hear every word that was said. The senator came furiously across the floor, saying: "Madam, don't you see I am fighting this bill through? I will work for you when the time comes."

"Yes, senator," said Jean, as frightened as she had ever been at a wild Indian on the Umpqua; adding, "I wish you would write your name on my card introducing me to the president."

"*Me* introduce you to the president!" he said, with fire flashing from his eyes, "I am *ten times* as big a man as the president *ever* was."

This electrified Jean; she had no more toadyism to greatness. In an hour's time she was chatting away with the president as familiarly as any old farmer. She told him what Conkling had said.

He laughed heartily, saying: "Did he say that?" He was not stung by it a particle, only good-naturedly amused.

This is history. Grant told Jean to say to any senator that required that much encouragement that he would not veto the bill, granting women land. He called his editor, introducing Jean; requested him to see that every courtesy was extended to Mrs. Reming personally, and the land law especially. "I am in favor of the land law and also in favor of better wages for women," he said, and to confirm it, he told a little incident that happened to him. "When I was a young man in the army, stationed at Vancouver, Oregon, with a hundred dollars a month salary from the government, one day, our servant, Kitty Mahoney, came to me asking to have her wages raised. 'Yes, how much more wages do you want Kitty,' said I. Hesitating a moment, she said, 'Well, sure, Patrick O'Finnigan, that made so much money in the mines, told me he would give me fifty dollars a month, as I am a good cook, you know, but I'd rather stay with you—I don't like to leave Mrs. Grant and the childer.' 'Oh, well, Kitty, that is more than I can pay you, you go right to Mr. Finnigan, and I'll help Mrs. Grant do the work myself.' The girl went, and we were without a servant during the rest of our stay at Vancouver.' Then President Grant took a piece of paper, saying: "The greatest objection to women's taking up public lands, is the isolation that it will subject them to, but that can be overcome in this way," marking out a section thus, the dots indicating where the cabins might stand for mutual protection and society. "Show this to any objecting senator, and say that I drew the diagram for you," he said. "I will do anything in my power to assist you in securing the land law for women;" adding: "As this is your first visit to the capitol, perhaps you would like to see the conservatory, where there are several new plants," and calling a man, he requested him to show Jean through the grounds. The plants looked meager, and somewhat dwarfed, compared with the wild grandeur of the trees and flowers of the Pacific Coast, though they were the pride of the capital, and thousands of dollars had been spent on their cultivation.

After spending a few weeks at the capital, Jean returned home to the bosom of her family, who were as rejoiced to meet her as though she had been a man, away improving her mind in research and travel, and working for the public good. The Miser children declare no law ever divorced them from their mother. Time obliterates grief as well as joy, and thus we leave Jean and Mr. Reming as happy a pair as ever were mated, surrounded by their merry, promising children, enjoying the blessings of their California home.

Our next volume will give a full account of the chief characters in the story, excepting those who have gone to the other side and left us no direction.

THE END.

www.ingramcontent.com/pod-product-compliance
Lightning Source LLC
Chambersburg PA
CBHW032141230426
43672CB00011B/2410